The Time Mom Met Hitler, Frost Came to Dinner,

and I Heard the Greatest Story Ever Told

The time Mom met Hitler,

Frost came to dinner, and

I heard the Greatest Story ever told

a memoir

DIKKON EBERHART

Tyndale House Publishers, Inc.
Carol Stream, Illinois

Visit Tyndale online at www.tyndale.com.

TYNDALE and Tyndale's quill logo are registered trademarks of Tyndale House Publishers, Inc.

The Time Mom Met Hitler, Frost Came to Dinner, and I Heard the Greatest Story Ever Told: A Memoir

Designed by Jacqueline L. Nuñez

Edited by Jane Vogel

Published in association with the literary agency of D. C. Jacobson & Associates LLC, an Author Management Company. www.dcjacobson.com.

Library of Congress Cataloging-in-Publication Data

Eberhart, Dikkon.
    The time mom met Hitler, Frost came to dinner, and I heard the greatest story ever told : a memoir / Dikkon Eberhart.
        pages cm
    Includes bibliographical references.
    ISBN 978-1-4143-9984-3 (sc)
1. Eberhart, Dikkon. 2. Authors, American—20th century—Biography. I. Title.
    PS3555.B463Z46 2015
    813'.54—dc23
    [B]   2015002513

Printed in the United States of America

21	20	19	18	17	16	15
7	6	5	4	3	2	1

This memoir is dedicated to my poet father.

Dad's sense of humor is shown by his reaction to the Greek philosopher

Plato, who famously kicked all poets out of his perfect Republic.

Plato kicked all poets out of his perfect Republic because the

fire of their verses showed their closeness to divine ecstasy.

Closeness to divine ecstasy, Plato believed, was

dangerous to his settled Republic.

"Probably a good thing, after all," said Dad.

"We're devil and angel," he sighed, "devil and angel."

PROLOGUE

I woke up.

It was Sunday. It was March. It was windy and cold on the coast of Maine.

I had no idea how to solve my problem.

"I guess I'll try the church across the road this time," I said to Channa, my wife. I sighed. "There's got to be an answer. Somewhere there's got to be an answer."

Channa was still in bed. She was propped against pillows with a coffee cup and a book. She pulled the blankets higher. Her glance was affectionate but without anticipation.

"You go. I'm too shy."

"Shall I need a tie, do you suppose?"

"This is Maine."

I swung out of bed. The floor was cold. I hurried to dress—collared shirt but no tie. From up the road, the church bell rang.

"Tell me all about it," Channa said.

"Back soon." I bent and kissed her. "How long can one more church service take, after all?"

I went downstairs. I didn't see the children. Someone had eaten cereal and not cleaned up afterward.

I was too tense to eat.

I pulled on a winter coat and stepped out the door.

Watch out!

Here comes the Jew.

PART ONE

CHAPTER ONE

I am Adam Eberhart.

At least, that's who I was in utero.

Then, on the way to the hospital in Boston, my mother—who knew her husband well—asked my father one last time if he wanted to change his mind, to which Dad replied, "Well, if it's a boy, I guess we'd better name him after me."

So instead of being Adam Eberhart—which is primary, euphonious, and individual—I became Richard Butcher Eberhart, son of Richard Ghormley Eberhart.

When I was brought home, Dad and our next-door neighbor were philosophizing upon the event.

"What will you call him?" our neighbor wanted to know.

My father was Richie to my mother and close relatives, and Dick to everyone else. So those names were used up. "How about Little Richard—but in Middle English: Diccon?" Dad suggested.

The neighbor, who was a Greek scholar, scribbled on a piece of paper, considered it for a moment, and then said, "The name would look better, aesthetically, if you used the Greek *k* instead of the English *c*. Thus: Dikkon."

And so it was.

Not a great name when you are in junior high. You can imagine the taunts. So I was Richard in seventh grade and Rick in eighth and ninth grades. Dad's academic-gypsy life gave me the liberty to remake myself with abandon every time I changed to a different school. (I attended seven of them during twelve years.)

During my seminary years, people often misunderstood me to be "Deacon" Eberhart, which, while it led to a funny explanation, did little to affirm my sense of identity. During the 1970s, when I was living in Berkeley, the daikon (a Japanese radish) rose to prominence, leading people to wonder if perhaps *that* was how my name was supposed to be pronounced. (So you'll know, it's pronounced *Dick-On*.)

Try introducing yourself as Dikkon Eberhart at a noisy cocktail party. What people hear is aggressively German—Dick von Eberhart.

Later, during my career as a salesman, I discovered that my name was a benefit after all. Customers often forgot my name after a sales call, but they *did* remember that they liked to buy from that salesman with the strange name. They would call my employer. *Send me the guy with the odd name.*

During Shakespeare's time, Diccon was a famous character in many plays about bedlam—madness. Diccon was used by many playwrights as a disruptive trickster, who stole and jabbered and kept the farce moving along, presumably to laughter and to ridicule from the audience. And in Shakespeare's own *Richard III* that wicked king is called Dickon by his scheming supporters.

These were not the sorts of Dikkon I desired to be. When I was young, though, Mom introduced me to a different sort of Dickon—in Frances Burnett's *The Secret Garden*. Burnett's Dickon is a wild boy from the moors—yes, as he sometimes was in the bedlam plays—but here, Dickon is also a spiritual guide. It is Dickon who assists Colin and Mary in the secret garden and helps them to heal.

At last! Here was a namesake who was neither a bedlam trickster nor a humpbacked king who may have smothered his own nephews (and did, according to Shakespeare). A vast improvement. I must have read that salubrious book a dozen times while growing up.

During the years when separating myself from my father was a big issue for me, I used to long after that fellow Adam. I had almost escaped! Surely Adam would not have had any of the problems Dikkon had!

You see, my father was a poet, and he was very well received—indeed, famous—in America and England during the half century between the early 1930s and the late 1980s. My parents knew and were close friends with most of the poets who were publishing during those years—Robert Frost, Dylan Thomas, Allen Ginsberg, T. S. Eliot, W. H. Auden, Robert Lowell . . . the list is long. Most of these people were casual droppers-in at our house, largely, I believe, because my parents were cordial and were pacifists when it came to literary war.

Dad and Mom delighted in almost every poetical voice, regardless of who had recently snubbed whom, or whom the critics were making eyes at just then. The critics appoint themselves to be the door wardens to literary immortality—they hold the keys to what many poets want most. The struggle for approval by the critics might simmer for years, as one group seeks to advance in critical attention against another group.

Literary battles can be fierce, but some of them provide us with great one-liners. For example, when I was young, debate had been ongoing for decades about the value of what is called *free verse*. Writers of free verse avoid conventional structures of poetry such as rhyme and meter and punctuation and any set length of line. Instead, they write their verse in open form anywhere on the page and believe they have creatively freed both themselves and their readers from stodgy old constraints in favor of greater beauty and inspiration.

One of Dad's friends, Allen Ginsberg, was often looked upon as a master of free verse. Several times I heard Allen proclaim his allegiance to free verse. But another friend of Dad's, Robert Frost, came up with the best line. Frost said that writing free verse is like playing tennis without a net.

Granted, many a young man has a father who looms large in his life, particularly in his early life. I became aware of Dad's professional success later—the prizes, the awards, the laureateships, the honorary degrees, his many books, etc. What I was aware of as a boy, however, were his passionate words themselves—their hot rhythms and their vibrant inflections.

Dad was an ardent lyricist. When Dad read his poems aloud (or rather *sang* them, as I thought it), his particular words, in their particular order, seemed to me to have hung in the air forever, indelibly, from the moment of Creation itself. This impressed me mightily. In our living room, or from a stage somewhere, there came cosmological and literary perfection, and it was modeled for me by my dad.

If I had been a different boy (if I had been Adam, for example), my life would have been easier. For if I had been a different boy, I might have aspired to be an astronaut, or a quarterback, or an FBI agent, or something else—certainly not a poet! But in my soul, I knew that I was like Dad. I, too, was a word-smithing guy.

And Dad . . . well, Dad cast a decidedly long literary shadow.

From the day I was born, from the very giving of my name, I had been molded as a literary artifact. Perhaps that moment with Dad and our Greek-scholar neighbor was like what happened in Eden when God paraded His newly created creatures before Adam to get their names.

What shall we call this new thing, and why? That was the question God asked of Adam.

Adam said, *It's a dog! Because he is loyal and brave and will fight for us.*

Dad (and his friend) said, *It's a Dikkon! Because he shall absorb his father into his very soul on the chance that one day, like a chrysalis, he may emerge from his cocoon with his own wider and radiant wings.*

I was—at once—positioned for literary potential, yet at the same time saddled by Dad's own literary achievement. It was a weight under which I would stagger and chafe for decades.

Without intending it, my father and his Greek-minded friend had sentenced me to a lifetime of worry and self-doubt. I could never claim victory in the war I launched against myself to defeat that doubt. I was much like another Greek, the mythical King Sisyphus, who was sentenced by Zeus to spend eternity pushing a giant boulder up the side of a mountain, only to have it roll back down again each time the boulder was just inches from the top.

Growing up, I sat at our dining table with literary "gods"

beside me, and I passed the peanuts to them at cocktail parties. I delighted to run in my imagination, to catch up with their quick talk and with their perfected allusions. I was aware that I was not *of* them, yet I observed that my parents delighted in them. I thought that someday I might word-smith, too, and then I would be *of* them.

They impressed me, not because of their literary renown—I was indifferent to that because they all had literary renown in the same way that they all had faces or feet—but because of their oddities.

The seemingly delicate poet Marianne Moore excited me with her baseball interest—and was chosen later to throw out the first pitch during the 1968 baseball season at Yankee Stadium.

The urbane southern poet Allen Tate delighted me when he argued at length with Dad about the language of human sexual intercourse. Is it *always* making love (Tate's view) or can it legitimately be described as . . . well, a word with an *f* (Dad's view). Vital info for me at fifteen!

The Majorcan poet, novelist, and mythologist Robert Graves—in the States to assist the filming of his Roman novels *I, Claudius* and *Claudius, the God*—who declined to discuss with me his experiences in World War I, and wanted instead to laugh with Mom and Dad about the unhappy fate of his bohemian grocery store—he was amusing both for his erudition and for his mouse-skin cap.

The tweedy Sir Osbert and the long-nosed Dame Edith Sitwell—she with the diamonds as big as ice cubes on her fingers—excited my imagination. Though brother and sister, they were my first knight and lady. Dame Edith asked novelist

Evelyn Waugh to be her godfather when she converted to Roman Catholicism. The author of *Brideshead Revisited*, Waugh was a favorite of mine.

Angular Ted Hughes and pretty but strained Sylvia Plath were, after Plath's suicide, the protagonists in a literary and feminist furor over the contents of Plath's roman à clef *The Bell Jar*. I remember Hughes, not Plath, although I probably met her because she was a Cambridge-based, literary-minded, Smith College girl not unlike my mother, although eighteen years her junior. What I do remember is my parents' concern for them at the incautious shortness of time between their meeting and their marriage—only four months.

Encounters like these were endless, but I could empathize with poor old King Sisyphus. It's no small task perpetually breaking bread with greatness, trying to keep up with greatness's chatter, but coming up short of it time and time again.

Greek mythology also tells us that King Sisyphus was guilty of murder.

For years, I believed I was too.

Here's what happened.

CHAPTER TWO

Dad was born in 1904, in Austin, Minnesota, the seventh generation of Eberharts in America. We count our line as commencing with Paul Eberhart, who was born at sea in 1727, while his parents were en route from what is now Germany to Philadelphia. As was the case with most eighteenth-century immigrants, the Eberharts came to this country for greater civil and religious freedom and for greater financial opportunity than they had in the Old World.

They emigrated from Wurttemberg, which is now part of Germany, anchored by its capital city, Stuttgart. If you go to Stuttgart today, you will find statues there of our ancestors, among them Eberhart the Noble, Eberhart the Groaner, Eberhart the Fat, and—this is the one I like the best—Eberhart of the Rushing Beard.

Once our family came to the New World, we pressed ever westward from Philadelphia through western Pennsylvania, Illinois, and finally into Iowa.

Dad's grandfather was Jeremiah Snyder Eberhart, a Great

Plains circuit-riding Methodist preacher possessed of—it was said—a fiery passion. Jeremiah had three brothers who were ministers too. One of those minister brothers was Isa Eberhart, who also became a published poet. So when Dad was a young teenager and the assignment at school was to produce a poem by the next day, and in an ecstasy of excitement, Dad produced *five* poems, the Eberhart family's explanation was that, of course, Dad was merely following the lead of his great-uncle Isa, the minister-poet.

My father's father was born in Albion, Iowa, about sixty miles west-northwest of Cedar Rapids. His full name was Alpha LaRue Eberhart, but he was always known by his initials, as A.L.

During A.L.'s youth, there was virtually nothing in northern Iowa and southern Minnesota save for acre upon acre of black-earth prairie, on which the American Indians had once resided along with flights of killdeer and herds of buffalo. At first slowly, and then with greater rapidity, frontier homesteading farmers arrived, which meant that towns were built, churches were planted, entrepreneurialism flourished, the law made its first inroads, and a rough-and-ready frontier ethos became the norm.

In this way, the American prairie was tamed and usefully transformed—as the nineteenth century would record it—into the production of wheat, corn, alfalfa, soybeans, and especially of hogs, steers, and chickens.

There were a lot of hungry mouths in the cities of the East, and those mouths needed to be fed. That need created a generation of strong farmers on the Midwest plains, who plowed, and harrowed, and winnowed, and threshed. It was a time when young men weighing no more than one hundred pounds came of age by mastering two thousand–pound Percheron horses—sometimes, indeed, four of them at the same time. The terrain was flat and vast. Young men were out there alone on the land, controlling their teams with the flick of reins and a whistle.

A.L. left school at age fourteen and began his career as a farm laborer. But he had bigger ideas than that. Chicago was the place where a young man with drive could succeed, and so, a year later, A.L. made his way there. During the next six years, he managed to save enough money to open his own store, selling men's fashions. But he was too restless for retail, and he sold the store and went out on the road as a glove salesman.

The financial panic of 1890 drove A.L. back to Chicago, where he capitalized on what was a family acquaintance with George H. Swift. Swift brought the young Eberhart into the Swift meatpacking company, and over the next few years A.L. rose until he was a manager of Swift's South St. Paul, Minnesota, branch.

By 1900, A.L. had made a name for himself—he possessed energy, drive, imagination, and the hunger to live well. The late nineteenth century created an opportunity for many men to get rich. One of them was a New York–born German butcher named George A. Hormel. Any man with the ability to catch a wind as it blew—and with the vision to sail it cunningly—could make the prairie hum. George A. Hormel was one such man.

By the time of my father's birth, Austin, Minnesota, was humming. There, in 1894, Hormel had begun to build his dream of a meatpacking enterprise that could rival George Swift's. He had assistance from his three brothers, but most especially, in 1900, he seduced A.L. away from Swift. Hormel knew a comer when he saw one, so he brought my grandfather aboard as a director and made him head of sales, and in 1901, they incorporated.

Two years later, A.L. and his wife, Lena, celebrated the birth of their first son, Dryden. Then, in 1904, their second son, my father, was born; their daughter, Elizabeth, came a few years later. Everything was falling into place for A.L. and Lena. By the time my father was born, A.L. was on his way to becoming a wealthy man.

A.L. could help people decide. Every business needs people to decide. A *yes* helps the business and the customer directly. A *no* may help the competitor, which in the end helps the business by forcing it to improve. But a *maybe* is death. A.L. was a no-maybes guy. And as it turned out, the apple didn't fall far from the tree.

Uncle Dry also became a salesman (stocks and bonds), as did his son, Bill (cosmetics). For a brief period in his forties, even Dad spent time as a salesman (floor wax). Unlike the others, though, Dad held on to his sales job only until something better came along. Unlike his father, Dad was *not* a no-maybes guy. Dad was a poet. Poets love maybes. A poet's maybe is the linguistic and aesthetic well from which creative juices flow. If you want to find the home of a poet's muse, figure out the location of that poet's maybe.

* * *

Soon after my father was born, the Eberhart family moved into Burr Oaks, an eighteen-room home (complete with a basement bowling alley, basketball court, and dance hall) that A.L. built for his growing brood and that dominated forty acres of fields, woods, and scrub between itself and the Cedar River. Many are the youthful adventure stories that Dad set there.

In the melt days of early spring, Dad and his brother, Dry, would chop enormous cakes of ice loose from the river banks and launch them into the stream. They'd take big branches of downed trees aboard, and using these clumsily for oars, they'd try to maneuver their unsteady craft downstream. The river was cold, and though it was not deep in summer, in spring its current ran very high and fast with the snowmelt water, and once it entered the woods, its way was tangled with fallen trunks and rock outcrops. The goal was to ride the urgent current all the way to the falls . . . of course, when no one was looking—no parent, that is—for this was a daring and dangerous thing to do.

When I was young and enthralled with the stories Dad would tell, the Cedar seemed to me to be as wild as Huck Finn's river, and just as fine a place for a boy to lie on his back, adrift upon a raft, and to feel that the world is, indeed, awful purty.

"Tell the one about the ice cakes," I'd plead. Then I'd snuggle against my father, he of the scratchy face and pipe smoke. For I was little, and he was big, and I'd know the story would come out okay.

As the boys float along, the day grows colder, and it begins to snow. And the trees close in. It's darker. And the river runs faster now as it dips into the darkness of the forest. And there are—of course—the falls ahead. Not yet heard, but waiting, dark and toothed. Then, in the dark: a lurch. The ice cake hits a fallen tree, rides up a little, whirls, hangs precariously, and . . . cracks in half! Plunges into the stream. The boys are wobbling now, crouching, terrified. Another piece of ice breaks off. Water covers the top of the ice now. Now they're

sinking. And now they hear . . . is that the falls? It is!
And now the falls are closer. And no one knows where
they are. Faster the river runs, and faster. The falls are a
roar. The ice cake whirls. Then, just at the penultimate
moment, the boys spy a tree branch hanging low across
the stream. Can they make it? Frantic work with the
useless oars. Closer. Closer. The falls are a death trap
about to snap closed. The boys crouch. They spring.
They clasp. They sway. The ice cake disappears in a
rumble of destruction. And there are the boys hanging
by their armpits, shuffling sideways, immortal.

Ah, the thrill! And it *might* have happened. One can never really
be sure with poets.

* * *

My mother found an attractive, frontier, Tom Sawyer–ish quality
in Dad's tales of his Minnesota youth. Of course when Dad was
young, the unfenced prairie no longer stretched from southern
Minnesota all the way to the Rockies. But Mom, who grew up in
cultured surroundings in Cambridge, Massachusetts, was nonetheless thrilled with Dad's vicarious touches of the Wild West.

My mother was a woman who loved to sing her way around
the house as she swept and cooked, and a particular favorite
was Bing Crosby's hit "Don't Fence Me In." She and I would
do the song together in the kitchen as she prepared onions, a
slice emphasizing the end of each line—

I want to ride to the ridge where the West commences [slice]
And gaze at the moon till I lose my senses [slice]

And I can't look at hobbles and I can't stand fences [slice]
Don't fence me in [sweep everything into the pot]

I understood Mom's delight at the idea that her husband, when he was a boy, might have ridden his cayuse all the way to the mythical spot where the West commences. Mom loved Dad's frontier boyhood, just as she did his deeply expressed love of the history of his family.

Family lineage, the dignity of earliest ancestry—these were very important to my father. He thrived on the meaning of being an Eberhart. Dad's mythmaking imagination delighted in *who we are*. Westward drive was one of the meanings of the American Eberharts.

But Dad had reversed the westward-pushing trend of our ancestors. While Uncle Dry settled in Wilmette, near Chicago, and Aunt Bunny (Dad's sister, Elizabeth) married a Texas oilman and settled in Albuquerque, Dad turned back to the east—first for his college education, then even farther to England for his graduate work. Upon returning to the States, Dad cemented our family's geography by making his living teaching at eastern universities and summering in Maine.

Why this reversal, undermining as it did a major Eberhart meaning? Because everything changed for my father when he was seventeen.

It was the fall of 1921. That was the time of the knockout punch. Dad's family was smacked down onto the mat, and when Dad looked up and shook his head to clear his buzzing brain, he perceived that everything had changed. Everything he had known and trusted had changed to a wilderness of doubt and fear.

CHAPTER THREE

So what happened in 1921?

To understand what happened, you need to know the three top men at Hormel. There was George A. Hormel, of course, whose dream it was to beat George Swift in business. There was A.L., his second-in-command, and there was Ransom J. Thomson, also known as Cy, who was comptroller and reported directly to my grandfather.

In 1921, A.L. was at the top of his powers. He was well respected in the meatpacking industry for his business acumen, and he was well compensated by Hormel for his sales success. A big man with a big car was my grandfather, and he supported his family with self-confidence.

Both Hormel and my grandfather were important men in the upper Midwest, and for a short period of time, Cy was too. Though he was still in his twenties, Cy was a friend of the governor, of senators and representatives, and of all persons of consequence in the region. He came to Hormel right after high school graduation and impressed George greatly with his drive and ambition.

He did not begin to steal until 1911.

Ten years later, in 1921, the story of Cy Thomson's million-dollar embezzlement was a national sensation. There was a Robin Hood fascination about the thing, owing in part to the fact that he gave a lot of the money away. Also, there was the local horror that this man—this man!—known and liked by everyone, the benefactor of thousands, was a crook! How could that be?

When Thomson returned after almost ten years in prison, many people stood him drinks, and clapped him on the back, and swore they had never believed in his guilt. His confession, they assured him, must have been a cover-up for the guilt of his superiors, one of whom was my grandfather, A.L.

So how did Thomson work it?

Once he was released from prison, Thomson wrote a memoir of about seventeen thousand words in which he sought to do three things. One, he addressed young men and warned them not to do what he had done. They must not find themselves "sinking into the quicksand," as he called it, of crime. Two, he explained that the embezzlement was really the fault of the Hormel organization because the Hormels had given such a young man as he was such ready access to the company's enormous funds (in 1920, Hormel grossed about $30 million). So, really, the incautious Hormels ought to have expected something bad to happen. And, three, he described how the embezzlement was done: he kited checks.

As Thomson said in his memoir, it was all so foolishly easy. The money was coming in so fast and moving around so fast, that no one except himself—and he did all this in his head without ever writing anything down—no one except himself could keep track of it, certainly no auditor. The downside for poor Thomson personally, though—and he bemoaned this in his memoir—was that he was losing sleep while trying to keep the accounts straight in his head.

The other downside was that he could never—not ever—take a day off. The entire community admired Thomson's attendance record at Hormel. What an employee this man was! He was tireless. He was faithful. He was always there with a ready answer anytime anyone asked a financial question. And every single day, after Thomson's Hormel work was done, he traveled the two hours to a spot next to the town of LeRoy, where he had laid out and was building his experimental farms and his entertainment park, Oak Dale. Every day, he oversaw its gargantuan growth.

Of course, the truth was that Thomson could never dare to miss a work day at Hormel because he couldn't risk someone else opening the mail.

Thomson's first theft was this: he stole $800 from a woman in South Dakota who mailed a check to the company to purchase eight shares of stock. Thomson issued the stock immediately. Then he placed her funds "in transit," as he said. That same $800 was still in transit ten years later when Thomson was finally found out.

The whole Cy Thomson story was—and remains—fascinating, in a fascination-with-depravity kind of way. For ten years, Cy Thomson was one of the biggest men in the upper Midwest. His Oak Dale enterprise was so famous that it attracted as many as thirty thousand eager visitors each weekend, at the cost of one dime per head.

So eager were the visitors to come to Oak Dale that the

famous Oak Dale Trail was carved out of the prairie. The Trail led travelers the 350 miles from Chicago, or the 180 miles from Minneapolis/St. Paul—to Oak Dale. Thomson published brochures and maps of the route, with notes suggesting stops at such-and-such a hotel, or restaurant, or campsite, or mechanic along the way. The cost to advertise in the brochure was to pave a section of the Trail. Each business that paved the Trail received a special Oak Dale Trail sign. Therefore, Thomson's customers experienced a smoothly paved road maintained at the expense of the advertisers (with frequent brand-name signage), and reassuring accompanying notes in the travel guide, which, among other enticements, listed the locations of all the most comfortable bathrooms along the nearly 530 miles of the Trail.

Why, the travel experience was as much fun as being at Oak Dale itself!

Cy Thomson began his experimental farms with Single Comb White Leghorn chickens and then branched out to Duroc hogs. But how to attract more customers? Beyond offering a tour of his barns—principally fascinating to the men of the visiting family—Thomson knew that he needed to attract the wives. The answer was Oak Dale Park.

As he did with everything, Thomson made the park grand. It had a pavilion dance hall decorated by the finest artist from San Francisco, with room for one thousand dancing couples and lit by two thousand electric lights. Famous bands such as Guy Lombardo, Lawrence Welk, and Red Nichols and His Five Pennies all played at Oak Dale. Even Thomson's tennis courts were lit for nighttime play. All you had to do was put a coin into the slot, and the lights came on for as long as the timer ticked. If you wanted more time, you just added more coins.

The simplicity was brilliant. Cy provided the lights. His customers paid the electric bill.

There were gymnasiums for children, wading pools, swings and slides, all surrounded by a fence so weary mothers could relax in the assurance that their little charges could not wander off.

And of course, there was also a large outdoor swimming pool.

I can imagine the Eberhart children at Oak Dale. There's my father—I can see him now—standing on the edge of the big swimming pool, which was a bright sheet of water, with all his friends in it, beckoning.

Cannonball!

Cy Thomson made all of this pleasure available to the upper Midwest during his ten short years of success. But Thomson's time was running out. In late 1920, an auditor from Minneapolis made a sudden appearance at Hormel, demanding to see the books immediately. The only mention of my grandfather in Thomson's memoir comes when Thomson convinces the auditor to go out with Mr. Eberhart for a round of golf and a luncheon at the country club before he sits down to the books. Had the auditor not joined A.L. during that morning, though the books would have looked fine on examination, the auditor would almost surely have noticed that Thomson was personally short by roughly $200,000 that day. But he did join my grandfather for a round of golf, and in that time, Cy managed to doctor the books in his favor.

Then in late April 1921, the Shawmut Bank in Boston wrote to Thomson asking why Hormel's cash position, recorded at slightly over $1 million, did not actually have $1 million of cash in it. Thomson was able to deflect the bank's concern by his usual subterfuge. However, the end was near. In early July

1921, the Shawmut wrote a letter directly to George Hormel in which it demanded a thorough examination of the company's books. Hormel gathered the directors and called Thomson into his office.

In Thomson's memoir he makes the exculpatory point that he did not really have the heart and soul of a thief—after all, it was the fault of the Hormels that he had had such ready access to their cash. And he proves his innocence of true thievishness to his readers by describing his thoughts during his perp walk down the hall to the office of the boss.

A real thief, Thomson avers, would have had the guts to concoct some alibi during that minute-and-a-half walk. But Thomson—obviously to himself not a real thief—merely opened the boss's door and before anything else could be said, blurted, "Gentlemen, it's all over; the jig is up."

One hour later, he wrote the last entry he would ever write in the company's general journal, an entry charging R. J. Thomson with $1,187,000—the exact total of the money he had embezzled during the ten years since he took $800 from an investor in North Dakota.

And in those days a million bucks counted for something.

Thomson cooperated with the lawyers and the accountants who were brought in; he showed them where every stolen dollar was. He signed over to Hormel every property he had ever bought with stolen funds, most of which Hormel liquidated quickly, and then Hormel turned to A.L.

One of A.L.'s principal assets was his stock position in Hormel. A condition of his contract provided that if danger to the company were dire, he could be forced to sell it back to the company for a fraction of its value. The embezzlement created such a condition. Meanwhile, the banks wanted a clean slate. No charges were brought against A.L. related to the embezzlement. However, the bankers, and perhaps Hormel himself, wanted Eberhart gone. Grandfather had shared an office with Thomson, and there were those who felt he must have been aware of what transpired, or at the least, that he had failed to exercise due diligence. He was, after all, superior to the crook. He was second in command at Hormel. It had been his duty to keep a sharp eye.

Too, A.L. was not a Hormel. This was a family company, after all, and my grandfather was not part of the inner circle, whatever his value and skills. The company had just been dealt its most dangerous blow, and it was fighting for its very existence. It needed to concentrate on what was most precious. Eberhart, for all his good qualities, was not indispensable. And in any event, the Hormels could get their stock back, cheap.

How badly, in the end, was Hormel hurt? By September, Thomson was in Stillwater prison serving a fifteen-year term. Oak Dale Farms and the Oak Dale Park were owned by Hormel. A.L. Eberhart's stock position was restored to company control. And Jay Hormel, son of George, is reported to have said to the mayor of Le Roy that the embezzlement, which was a national media circus fueled by its Robin Hood appeal and carried in 1,300 papers across the United States, provided a bonanza in free publicity.

A.L. was in his midfifties at the time. He had worked for Hormel for twenty-one years. He was a man at the height of his powers. He was well respected by his peers elsewhere in the industry, and that proved to be a good thing. After my grandfather was let go at Hormel, George Swift, creator and president of Hormel's principal competitor, Swift Foods, handed him a blank check—literally: a signed check with no amount written in—and told A.L. that anything he needed was his.

At the same time A.L. was reeling from the financial blow, it became apparent that Lena was seriously ill. The word *cancer* was scarcely used around the household, and of course, never in front of the children. However, it was cancer—lung cancer (though my grandmother did not smoke)—and it weakened her inexorably during that dire summer of 1921. In the end, though, the truth could not be kept from the children, and A.L. took them to the apple orchard and laid it all out before them.

According to Dad, "Apple Orchard," a section of one of his longer poems, *Burr Oaks*, is an accurate rendition of the event. The beauty of the sun shining through the white-and-pink apple blossoms contrasts, both in the poem and in Dad's telling, with the ache of what needed to be told.

Dad was seventeen. Having just graduated from Austin High School, he decided to postpone his departure for the University of Minnesota to assist with his mother's care and his sister's comforting. My grandmother was a believer in the power of prayer, and my father, his father, and she spent many hours together, praying. Other times, Dad read to her from uplifting books. He nursed her with tender bites of food when she could eat, and with drinks of tea or lemonade. He also managed and monitored visitations from other ladies of the town. Sometimes Lena was simply too weak to accept a visit, and Dad acted as her secretary, politely offering apologies on her behalf.

Eventually, there came a time when prayer and local doctoring were of no avail, and the family accompanied Lena to Chicago to have what was then a last-resort therapy employing dangerous radiation. For a time, Lena showed improvement, and the family returned to Austin. However, Lena's recovery was short lived, and she died in November 1921.

When Dad would tell this tale to my younger sister, Gretchen, and me, he would use a tone that lent the tale a sense of awe and of tragedy that endowed it with an almost Shakespearean aura— or at least it did for me. Of course, I was young, and I loved my dad. In reality, though the tale is colorful enough, it is really just an ordinary human tale of a business reversal coincident with a parental death.

Dad's journal entries from the period reflect the yearning he felt for her recovery and, more vaguely, for the recovery of his father's fortunes. The entries are articulate beyond the ordinary, even for a time when youngsters were more carefully schooled in English composition than they are today. Emerging in Dad's journal is a passionate voice. Dad was already a writer of poetry, but his journal marks the emergence of a powerful prose maker.

Many times, to me and to interviewers, Dad explained his poetic determination in life as "my attempt to heal a bifurcated and an inexorably anguished soul." His soul may have been bifurcated—cut in half—by the twin calamities which his family encountered, but there was another element in Dad's poetic determination that was apparent to me. It was apparent to me because I shared it. He was a Romantic. He believed in emotion as the great doorway to intense aesthetic experience, such a high level of experience that it closely touched the level of the divine.

1921. This is the time and these are the events that wounded my father, and he barely adjusted to it. Once, he told me it wasn't until he was in his fifties that he finally began to recover from the death of his mother. That's a long, long burn.

CHAPTER FOUR

Now for the other side.

My mother's grandfather invented floor wax.

When I was very young, it seemed odd to me that some person should have needed to invent floor wax in the first place. The stuff was ubiquitous; it was just around. It was as though someone's great-grandfather had needed to invent the fork or the chair.

Charles Butcher was an English immigrant and a finish carpenter. During the 1870s, he laid many of the parquet floors in the brownstones being built just then in the developing Back Bay section of Boston. The trouble was that the maids scrubbed his floors with soap and water, which made them whiten and splinter, or they rubbed them with beeswax, which made them sticky, particularly in hot weather. There had to be a better way.

Butcher lived in Cambridge, across the Charles River from Boston, and he experimented in his barn. Eventually, he discovered that a combination of carnauba wax, beeswax, turpentine, and other ingredients produced a hard, shiny, durable, and inexpensive finish, perfect for the protection and beautification of his floors. He took to handing out a can of Butcher's Boston Polish whenever he finished a floor job. In time, demand for his polish became so great that in 1880 he stopped doing floors and founded the Butcher Polish Company. During its next 120 years, the company existed as a private, family-controlled enterprise.

Charles Butcher, the inventor, had a son named Charles Howlett Butcher, who was my grandfather. This second Charles was brought in to the family business, and he lived in the little house right next to the factory, which was in the barn.

Not long after that, my grandfather married my grandmother, Margareta Magdalena Theresa Carstensen Butcher. So she had five names! What other young fellow had a grandmother with so suggestively regal an appellation . . . and who was so slender and so elegant and who spoke German and could sit on her hair?

Grandmother died two weeks short of her 102nd birthday. As we grandchildren were growing, and later when we were grown, Grandmother seemed, indeed, to be immortal. She scarcely seemed to change as the years went by. Unfailingly, she was generous of spirit toward her grandchildren, particularly with regard to birthday checks. As I noticed each of Grandmother's many generosities of spirit to me—her first grandchild—I cast on more of the stitches that knit me to her in a sweater of deepest love.

Grandfather handled the wax business and richly prospered; he was known in Cambridge business circles as the Polish King. He favored the Bull Moose Republicans, kept all of his workers employed even during the worst of the Depression, and refused to patent the Butcher's formula—"If someone else wants to make a living with wax, why should I stand in his way?" And according to my mother, Grandfather was not a man to raise a ruckus with his wife.

Butcher's Polish Company continued to thrive, and it continued to use the barn as its factory. When Mom was a girl, the factory was a small, creaky place, and it was just the same when I was a boy too. My pals and I were allowed to pour the cherished mixture into the vats, to paste the labels on the cans (often not very straight), and even to ride up and down the belt conveyor that lifted the cans up to the carriage loft.

The factory had another benefit for Mom. When she was a marriageable attraction around Cambridge, she used the factory as a way to weed out her beaux. Mom would bring some young Harvard Business School go-getter to see her family's factory. The suitors were aware that the Butcher Polish Company generated substantial livings for Grandfather and for his brother and cofounder, Uncle Will. At business school, the suitors had also been exposed to case studies of Butcher's competition. Butcher's competition employed many, many workers and had huge factories. Mom would laugh with me about these visits. "Some of the men could see that it took real business sense to make our sort of success from a factory in a barn and a laboratory in the cellar closet. But others were embarrassed for us. I learned something useful this way about the perspicacity of my beaux."

Of course, as I was growing up, we used Butcher's wax at our house. Those orange cans with their black lettering made me feel good. "Dikkon," my mother used to tell me as she waxed and as I enjoyed the smell, "my grandfather invented this—so it's yours, too."

I often made use of Butcher's wax myself. I liked to go to the hardware store and see whole shelves of Butcher's products on display. When I was a teenager, I would stand quietly in the wax department, with a finger on my chin, making myself a lure.

Of course, a clerk would rise to my bait. "May I help you?"

"I see you have a lot of Butcher's."

"Well, it's the best. Always has been. But I have some others down here too, if you are looking for something a little less costly."

"No, thanks," I would say loftily. "I always prefer quality. Quality is the most important." And then I would leave without buying anything, because after all, we had cases of quality at home.

The biggest fish I ever caught, however, was not landed at some mere hardware store. I caught my biggest fish when I was fifteen. Our family was enjoying a private tour of the White House, along with Grandmother, who had become the titular head of Butcher's after my grandfather died, although the company's day-to-day management and expansion was the work of Uncle Charlie, her son (and the third Charles).

Since it was a private tour, it must have been arranged by my father, who was Consultant in Poetry to the Library of Congress just then and could do so.

By the way, the current title of that job is Poet Laureate Consultant in Poetry to the Library of Congress and is commonly referred to as United States Poet Laureate. Dad's two-year appointment spanned the end of the Eisenhower administration and the beginning of the Kennedy administration.

The poet laureateship is a paid position without a job description. Here's the money; do whatever you want. Since 1937, when the position began, there have been forty-nine poets laureate. I have known twenty-four of them, some quite well—they were the men and women who trooped through our houses and for whom, as a teenager, I needed to be prepared at any moment to recite my Shakespeare. (Gretchen needed to be prepared to play the piano.)

Dad followed Frost. Frost had one year; Dad had two. The poet laureateship is the single paid position in the United States government honoring a person for mastery of any variety of art. The money for the position comes from a private foundation, not from taxpayers. What the laureate gets from the taxpayers is use of an office at the far end of an upper corridor in the Library of Congress's Jefferson Building—small, but with an inspiring view of the Capitol dome.

As poet laureate, Dad devoted his time to helping widen the Library of Congress's poetry collection, to bringing poets together for symposia, to hosting visiting poets from other countries, to answering poetry questions from schoolchildren and teachers, and to encouraging poetry curricula in schools.

But I digress.

Our tour of the White House included a stop in its vast, gleaming ballroom with its lovely hardwood floor. I was standing next to Grandmother, just inside the ballroom entrance, and we were all admiring the room's elegance and—I was, anyway—imagining the important dancers who, at some later time, would be keeping step to the music.

I turned to the tour guide and inquired, "How do you keep these floors so bright?"

He looked at me, perhaps startled by what was an unusual question from a teenage boy. "We can't endorse any product."

"Yes, of course. But what do you use to keep it bright, just out of curiosity?"

"Well, to satisfy your curiosity, of course we use the best there is. It's called Butcher's."

With a sweeping gesture, I indicated my grandmother. "May I present Butcher's chairman of the board?"

We all had a good laugh.

*   *   *

While the man who would become Dad's father-in-law successfully confronted the Depression and secured his own company, his employees, and his family, my father hid out from it. Not that I am disparaging him. I probably would have done the same. As the Depression deepened, Dad made an effort to earn a doctorate at Harvard, but the money ran out, and his father, who had always seemed to him invincible, was unable to help.

Regardless, nothing was going to get in the way of Dad's poetry—nothing. Yet without a Harvard PhD, he felt he was at a standstill. While other writers of the time cast themselves on the roiling waters, sink or swim, Dad looked for a shore on which he could sit and contemplate the storm. And because he was Dad, he found one. Or rather, one found him.

In 1932, St. Mark's, a boys' prep school in Southborough, Massachusetts, offered Dad a decent wage, room and board, and time to write, in exchange for teaching freshmen and sophomores about English literature.

Among Dad's students were Robert Lowell (forever known as Cal for his brilliant acting of the part of Caligula at St. Mark's), who, like Dad, would go on to be United States Poet Laureate and would win the Pulitzer prize, our nation's most prestigious literary award, twice to Dad's once; and Ben Bradlee, future editor of the *Washington Post*, who gained international fame when he challenged the federal government over what he took to be the paper's right to publish the "Pentagon Papers" (classified national security documents detailing secret enlargement of the scope of the Vietnam War by the government) and who later oversaw Bob Woodward and Carl Bernstein's articles burrowing into the Watergate scandal, the investigation of which led to the impeachment of President Richard Nixon.

Of course, compared to many poets who were Dad's contemporaries, Dad's life in general and his choice of a way to work during the Depression were socially acceptable. Many poets of that time eschewed conventional life. They hated the idea of work, of personal responsibility, of monogamous marriage, and the like. They were bohemians. Appalled at what capitalism had wrought, they thundered their disapproval in magazines.

For instance, W. H. Auden (who wrote, among other things, the oft-quoted poem "Funeral Blues," made famous in the film *Four Weddings and a Funeral*), despite living off Dad's goodwill at St. Mark's for several months, when departing, roared in fury, "For God's sake, Dick, get out!" Likewise, E. E. Cummings, the popular avant-garde poet and painter—who lived off his father, was drunk much of the time (Dad used to bring him bottles of milk to try to sober him up), and fathered a daughter with his best friend's wife—rigorously advocated to Dad freedom for poets from such dreary, conventional work as teaching.

But life at St. Mark's—conventional as it may have been—nonetheless provided Dad with a roof over his head, some money in his pocket, and most important, time to meet and to nurture his muse.

As it happens, it also provided him with a wife.

CHAPTER FIVE

My sister, Gretchen, and I exist because of our Uncle Charlie.

It was Charlie who introduced a bachelor English master at St. Mark's School in Massachusetts to his sister in October 1939. That year was Charlie's first as a math master at St. Mark's, having just graduated from Harvard. Dick Eberhart, who was making something of a name for himself as a poet, was twelve years Charlie's senior and had been teaching at St. Mark's for several years.

The two men struck up a friendship. When Charlie's birthday was approaching, and he learned his family was giving a small dinner in his honor, he said to his pal, "Why not come to our place in Cambridge? My sister will be there. You'll like her; she's smart." Then he wrote a note to his parents and to Heb (the family name for Helen Elizabeth Butcher—known to everyone else as Betty) saying he would be bringing a poet home for dinner.

A poet? my mother remembers saying to herself. *Some effete bohemian, no doubt. Not my type.*

Heb was twenty-five years old at the time, had graduated from Smith College, and had recently returned from Kentucky and the Frontier Nursing Service, where she had met, she used to laugh with me, the very type of the Hatfields and the McCoys—if not they themselves—while she rode through the mountains dispensing medicine and assisting in childbirths. Now she was back in Cambridge to take up a grade school teaching position and enroll at Simmons for a master's in sociology. Heb was short, wiry, jolly, interested in everything, and determined to make something of the world around her.

That was my mother in 1939. When she died in 1994, fifty-five years later, she was almost the same. Unhappily, she had deteriorated significantly, both mentally and physically, due to the epilepsy that manifested when she was in her forties. The condition, as well as the drugs she took to control it, wore her down. However, there were times when the flash of her spirit would break free, and I delighted once more to experience my mother as she had been.

*   *   *

By the time Dad met Mom, he had already strung together an impressive collection of worldly credentials. He knew England, Ireland, France, and Germany well, Italy less well, and he had worked his way on tramp steamers—westabout—from San Francisco to England. As an able seaman plying back and forth among various ports of the China Sea and the Southern Ocean, he had inhaled the gingered air of exotic anchorages. Beyond that, he had been awarded the Most Exalted Order of the White Elephant, Commander (Third Class), by King Prajadhipok of Siam, for services duly rendered. The order, established in

1861 by King Ramah IV, was awarded for meritorious service to the crown. Dad's honor—at the level of Commander of the Order—was the fourth highest among the levels. Having been awarded his ribbon, Dad knelt before the king, who then presented my father with the keys to the city of Bangkok.

Now, there are other American poets who have won the professional honors my father won—and more besides—but certainly, as his friend and fellow United States Poet Laureate Daniel Hoffman pointed out, Dad is the *only* major American poet who possesses the keys to the city of Bangkok!

This particular honor came to Dad after a successful stint as tutor to the prince of Siam. The tutoring assignment occurred at a vast estate north of New York City to which the king had repaired when it became clear that he needed to have a cataract removed. There was nowhere in his own country where such a thing could be done with the certainty of success due a king. So the king, the prince, and an entourage of more than one hundred courtiers descended on New York, where they remained for almost a year.

My father, recently returned to the States from Cambridge University in England, was at the moment "on his uppers," as he liked to tell me (which means broke)—though, as he chuckled, he looked grand, since he walked with a stick, wore spats, and smoked a meerschaum pipe. While broke, Dad's fallback job was at the Brooklyn slaughterhouses—"a very vision of hell"—and so he sought tutoring gigs fiercely. He had just completed a job tutoring the daughters of a millionaire manufacturer in Palm Beach, where, he said, "the girls were covered with a glaze like honey, and were stingless in the sun"—so tutoring the prince of Siam would be a coup.

The appointment carried Dad for almost a year. Once he had some money, he went back to Germany. It was 1931, and as a Commander of the Order of the White Elephant and a friend of the prince, Dad had entrée in Berlin to the Siamese legation. He attended all-night parties at the embassy, breakfasted with the prince on whiskey, wafers, and cigars exotically rolled in lotus leaves, and admired (from a distance) the fragile beauty of Siamese women while flirting with German women of more robust beauty.

But this was the 1930s, and Germany was suffering hyper-inflation while toying, in truculent vengefulness, with the fascism of this new man, Hitler. Dad was never politically astute (Mom was the political one in our house), but as some artists are, he was prescient and sensed an underlying menace.

So the poet who was to be presented at 117 Lakeview Avenue, Cambridge, and whom Heb feared was some effete bohemian, was not unaccomplished, nor did he lack prescience. Three weeks before Charlie's birthday party, Hitler invaded Poland, launching World War II.

Suddenly, *Blitzkrieg* was a new word on the American tongue. Before the invasion, Dad had joined a paramilitary unit out of Fort Devens, Massachusetts, which had been formed to prepare young professionals for military service if needed, and Dad spent a lot of time drilling and shooting.

Beyond that, Dad was succeeding as a poet. He had published poems in a number of leading magazines, particularly, in America, in Harriet Monroe's *Poetry*. In Britain, his was prominently the single American voice in the 1932 *New Signatures*.

New Signatures was an anthology, as it was presented as a sort of anti-Eliot publication—T. S. Eliot being the leader of the esoteric school of, as Dad used to disdain it to me, effete intellectual thinking. Dad was a feeler first, and while he liked Tom Eliot personally and was flattered by Eliot's interest in him, Dad thought that the man was literarily a cold fish. Here's how he summed up Eliot's work: "If you are writing only for those who may catch every recondite allusion in your footnotes—footnotes to a poem, forsooth!—then your audience is mandarin indeed."

The poets of *New Signatures* were introduced as passionate seekers for new ways to *feel* at a time when the coolness of technology was triumphant. W. H. Auden, Stephen Spender, Cecil Day Lewis—and Dad. Though Dad never considered them a "school," and though he never concerned himself very closely with the international social events that so deeply concerned the others—the Spanish Civil War, for example, or the triumph of Bolshevism and then Communism in Russia and Eastern Europe—for years afterward, Dad's name was bandied about with theirs as though they were a school.

Dad was on a roll—his poems appeared regularly in the establishment literary press. He had brought two volumes of his own poetry into being, *A Bravery of Earth* (1930) and *Reading the Spirit* (1936), and he had circled the globe. He had hobnobbed with writers, some of whom would later be giants, both in Europe and in America. And yet through all his travels, as he reported to me, my father had never seen a woman descend the staircase in her house to meet a visitor with the energy and with the vibrancy of Heb.

When Heb descended the stairs to meet this pal of her brother's, the bohemian poet, their eyes met, and he nodded. But he turned aside then and disappeared back into the library.

Heb stepped into the library in time to see the man draw up a cane from an umbrella stand and, continuing an interrupted conversation, lunge at her mother—a confirmed pacifist—as with a bayonet.

"Thus!"

"Yes, yes, Mr. Eberhart. But we'll never defeat Hitler *that* way."

"It's the only way."

Tableau.

The frisson passed—thank goodness—and soon after that Grandmother rang the bell and dinner was served. Later they all went to the theater to see *Life with Father*.

Heb wasn't beautiful, as Dad later confided to his brother in a letter; she was good looking, but it was the *life* in her that drew one.

For her part, my mother told me, she had always wanted a man with a soul. She had known many a world-beater in business as potential beaux—these were the fellows she weeded out at the factory—but she was drawn to a sensitive man. Trouble was, she was also a healthy young woman who disdained a wimp.

Her ideal, she reported to me, would be someone like her pal the painter Rockwell Kent, with whom she went to dances. He flattered her youthful infatuation, but he was clearly unsuitable by reason of both his age, which was advanced, and his radicalism, which was pronounced.

More suitable in terms of age was another of her dance favorites, Bradford Washburn, the mountaineer and later founder of Boston's Museum of Science, but that afternoon of Charlie's birthday, what Heb saw while she distracted the militarist poet from his attempted coup upon her mother was something that pleased her very much, right from the start.

Perhaps he did have a sensitive soul. But he also had the physique of a football player. He offered the straightforward, high-cheekboned, square-jawed visage of the American heartland. And soon she learned he was charm itself. "Not bad," she recalled to me years later. Even before dinner was served that evening, she had this idea—*Not bad at all.*

Of course, Heb's parents saw her attraction. Consequently, after she and my father had been for several long afternoon walks, her parents warned her that poets generally make very little money. At that time my father was waiting for pages of his newest book to be shipped from England for binding and publishing in the United States.

German U-boats were sinking a great many ships then, and Dad expressed his worry over the safety of his "sheets." Heb, who still did not know my father very well, was pleased to be able to relieve her parents' minds. Mr. Eberhart may have an avocation of poetry, she reported, but her parents would be pleased to learn that he had business sense as well—he was an importer of fine linens.

By the time that notion was dispelled, it was obviously too late to save Heb from her fate. She was in love and mightily so. Reciprocating the feeling, my father decided it was time to give Heb an important gift. At an auction, he bought her what he was told was a string of cultured pearls. Touched by the gift, Heb sent the pearls to a jeweler to be cleaned and restrung. When they were returned to her, they were accompanied by an appraisal identifying them as a perfect string of *natural* pearls.

Now, here's why my mother was, from the very first, a perfect mate for my father. Mom told me she never checked up on this discrepancy. It was more fun, she felt, *not* to know.

Were her pearls cultured, as Dad had paid for? Or had her string been switched by mistake at the jewelers with a much more valuable natural string? Or maybe the two *appraisals* had been switched by mistake? After all, pearls look pretty much the same, one from another, unless you're an oyster. Maybe now Mom really *did* have a valuable necklace of natural pearls, and someone else had her cultured ones—and neither of them would ever know! What fun!

But Dad was ever a diffident lover. He was good with a bayonet, with a pearl necklace, and with a poem, but he was hesitant—as it is said nowadays—about commitment. All through 1940 and halfway through 1941, Heb and Dick were inseparable. Frequently they discussed marriage. However, my father worried deeply that marriage might "kill off the poetry," as later he expressed it to me.

In July 1940, Dad took Heb to Chicago to visit his brother, Dryden, and Dryden's new wife, Dudie. During that visit, Uncle Dry took Dad aside and told him firmly that he must either marry the woman or set her free to pursue other marital opportunities, and that he, Dryden, would prefer the former. Meanwhile, Heb had begun to wonder whether her continued forbearance might imperil her dignity.

One afternoon, the two of them stopped their car beside Lake Michigan and had a very long talk that escalated into a furious row. At a certain point, Heb leaped from the car and disappeared into the shrubbery. My father sat in the car for a while, fuming, expecting her at any moment to return. When she did not return, he became worried, and he got out of the car and called for her and tried to find her among the shrubs. She was nowhere to be found. Increasingly frantic, Dad became convinced that, in her despair, she had thrown herself into the lake and had drowned.

That's the climax of the story as Dad always told it.

Now here's Mom's next chapter.

In fact, what had happened was that she had stomped along the shore until she found a bench in a park, and she had sat down there to cool off. When, to Dad's immense relief, he finally discovered her and explained to her how sure he had been that she was dead, she became so angry once more at his insufferable self-regard that she stated she was ending this cat-and-mouse game immediately and returning to Cambridge forthwith.

When Mom described this scene to me years later, it was not with the joking tolerance she generally used. Dad's unawareness of the simple play of human emotions and the actions they precipitated was then—and it remained—clouded by his poetical lens and by his conceit. And years later, even the memory of his blindness at so important a moment for my mother still hurt her.

Everyone was ganging up on poor Dad, and he had to do something.

So the next day, he invited Heb to attend a planetarium show before she departed. He had thought hard about this, and he had a poetical scene all planned. Under the skies of Mars and Venus, he intended to ask her his Big Question.

However, when they arrived at the Adler Planetarium, the place was closed. Dad was distraught. What was he to do? He couldn't just ask her his question as they sat in the car. Nor was a park bench the proper venue. As they strolled along the shore of the lake, his mind was casting frantically this way and that, while at the same time he was trying to give no clue of the turmoil inside. Soon they chanced upon a spot where one might take a speedboat ride onto the lake. Should she like to take such a ride? Well, yes. He paid, they clambered aboard along with a jolly crowd of other partygoers, the engines turned over, and the ride began. Then, at the moment when the boat reached its apogee into the lake, without a word—because he was too shy to have uttered one—he reached for her finger and slid onto it his mother's pearl ring set with diamonds.

Uncertain, hopeful, bruised, all Heb could say was, "But Richie, what does this *mean?*"

He was unable to do more than to nod.

However, the rest of the passengers got the point, and they began to cheer and clap.

It was good that they did, because at the moment, Dad, the passionate lyricist, could not voice anything at all. Later, when Dad would tell me this story and would arrive at this point, he would laugh. "I was speechless," he would say. "Isn't that amazing?"

CHAPTER SIX

Four months after my parents' marriage, the Japanese bombed Pearl Harbor. Dad wasn't certain what he must do. He had a responsibility to teach through that academic year at a high school in Cambridge, which he did. But what to do next?

It was late spring 1942, and the war was not going well. There were reversals on every front. With the exception of Jimmy Doolittle's symbolically satisfying but strategically insignificant bombing raid on Tokyo, the Japanese were implacable in the Pacific. Singapore fell. Rommel was rampant in North Africa. Tobruk fell. MacArthur's vow to return to the Philippines was moving, yet it seemed the merest braggadocio. Hitler's June invasion of Russia had stunned Stalin. The Wehrmacht was making mincemeat of the Soviets. The Allies appeared to be fumbling. They seemed to have no plan.

Dad's mind was frequently on the islands of the southwest Pacific, among which he had sailed with deep pleasure only fifteen years before, and he later told me it was easy to envision the horror there as the enemy overran the archipelagos. The Bataan Death March literally made Dad sick.

My father need not have enlisted. He was thirty-seven: too old. Indeed, most of his literary friends strongly discouraged him. The navy? That was no place for a poet. It would kill the muse. Had Dad no better idea what to do with his spirit than to fight a war? War was not for artists. War was for dumbbells. War was for those who had no subtlety, for those who could not see gray. Let others fight the war, stupid and blunt as it was.

In addition, Dad was confronted by the pacifism of his mother-in-law and by the conscientious objection of his brother-in-law. But Mom supported whatever Dad felt he must do, so when the spring semester was done, Dad applied for a commission in the navy as a deck officer. However, it turned out that he had red-green color blindness, a defect that excluded him from deck-officer training. In any event, he was a little too long in the tooth, so the navy routed him to the reserves, where his experience as a teacher and his skill with guns could be put to good use.

So while the battles raged abroad, he and my mother remained stateside—first in New Jersey, then Florida, and later California, until the war's end. Dad's duty was instructing in aerial free gunnery—teaching young men to shoot double-barreled machine guns from navy bombers. He was promoted several times and ended the war at Alameda Naval Air Station on San Francisco Bay.

As an aside, wherever he was stationed, Dad wrote. So much for killing the muse. It was the same with the business world: when Dad became a floor-wax salesman after the war, that, too, was supposed to be the death knell of his verse. But not so. Much of what I believe is Dad's best verse comes from the times when he thrashed for hours each day in the raw stew of life—and wrote at night, to restore his connection to God, or to joy, or at least to equilibrium.

Beyond Dad's writing, he had another asset wherever he was stationed. He had Mom. Often she would tell me that she and Dad had the best of it during the war. Most couples were separated, sometimes for months on end. My parents weren't. Dad was always pleased to have my mother along at officers' club parties so he could share a bit of her history. The talk might turn, let's say, to Hitler and to how that tyrant would respond to the anticipated cross-Channel invasion of Fortress Europe. That is, to D-day.

"Let's ask Betty," my father would say. "She knows Hitler."

Mom would respond with varying amounts of humor depending on the circumstance, "Oh, Richie, I don't *know* him. I *met* him."

And that was true. In 1936, when my mother had just graduated from Smith, her parents sent her, along with two classmates, on a trek to Europe, especially Denmark and Germany, to see cousins from my grandmother's side and, of course, castles and cathedrals.

Just then, some of Mom's German cousins were emigrating to America. For example, there was cousin Fritz Gynrod, the opera singer. Cousin Fritz would subject Mom to delicious embarrassment whenever she visited him in New York. He would stop her in the middle of a crowded sidewalk and burst into song, just to show her how *he* did that aria as compared with some other, competing singer. On the other hand, others among the Doerings and the Gynrods were staying in Germany. To Mom's disquiet, when she visited them, she found that some of them had even *voted* for Hitler. The man was, after all, keeping the Communists at bay.

(Later, after the war, it turned out that *none* of Mom's German cousins had voted for Hitler. In fact, it turned out that *nobody* had *ever* voted for Hitler, *ever*. Still, Mom used to chide them: "The man *told* you what he was going to do. All you had to do was read his book. He told you *in advance*."

"But we were frightened, Betty. Of the Communists we were afraid."

"You should have been afraid of yourselves!" Mom snapped.)

But in 1936, the girls had a splendid time touring Germany. Among other destinations, they went one time to Berchtesgaden. It was rumored that Hitler was there and was making himself available to the public. So they climbed up a long slope of alpine fields, lovely in the sunshine, in a slow-moving procession of the curious or the admiring. As they approached a flat near the summit, they descried a group of men in front of which the crowd was passing. The man in the middle, of average height and build, wearing a long overcoat, they determined must be Adolf Hitler. People would stop and speak with him, perhaps shake his hand, and then pass by.

As Mom approached Hitler, she struggled with what to say when she met the man. She disliked what little she knew of him, but her relatives thought he was doing well by them, and she hated to be impolite. Finally, she settled on "Greetings from America," in German. So when my mother met Hitler, she made a curtsy, straightened, and said her little speech. Hitler caught her eye, smiled slightly, nodded, and murmured thanks. Then my mother passed on.

Her two lasting impressions of her meeting with evil were

that the famous mustache fit his face much more naturally than it appeared to do in lampoons afterward, and that the men surrounding Hitler were so burdened with exotic armaments as to seem ludicrous.

Interesting stuff at the officers' club.

*   *   *

A thing that surprised me at first about Dad's reflections on the war was that the war had another side too. Everyone who has been in combat knows that war is hell. Even a noncombatant like my father knew this, he who at least had imagination.

But there is the love of war too, which is a puzzle for a poet. And war has its funny side. Dad saw the humor in it. One of the funny moments, he always said, occurred when the men didn't know whom to salute. You spend your entire professional life saluting everyone or being saluted by everyone else; it becomes an instinct. But what do you do when you can't tell whom to salute? For example, Dad used to laugh, whom do you salute in a communal shower? There may have been an admiral in there, and probably some captains, but who could tell? One tired body grabbing hot water and soap is much like another. And in any event, status in a shower among men is on a basis more ancient than gold braid.

Less frequently reported of war is the sorrow at war's end— that it is over. Many remember that photograph of the ticker tape and of that sailor kissing the girl in Times Square. But behind that happy picture is another truth: the war had given everyone something to do. Many people, especially young people, don't quite know what to do with their lives. They shamble; they lurch. War was good for some of them. Of course, war can be horrid, but for five whole years the war solved the problem for many young men and women who didn't know what to do. It had the ability to take them out of themselves—we were attacked; how can I help?

Nearly everyone had war work to do. As Dad pointed out to me, even someone who refuses a war must do war work. Uncle Charlie was a conscientious objector and as a result imprisoned, yet even Uncle Charlie had war work to do. First he needed to work to convince those who needed to be convinced that he *was* a conscientious objector. And then he worked a southern chain gang on roadsides, swinging a stunted scythe. Dad himself taught thousands of young men how to bring down the Zero, a Japanese fighter plane.

There were jobs aplenty, and while some of the work was stupid, and of course some of it deadly, any man or woman who could see beyond the screen of his or her personal interest had a welcome opportunity to do so.

Dad did classroom work, and there was the flying with his students so they could gain a feel of the gun positions and of the mechanics, but the most dramatic of his pedagogies was as follows. Dad stood behind a berm and flew eight-foot-tall kites with controllable rudders high in the air, while his students blasted live rounds into the image of the Zero silhouetted on them. Dad could control the kites intricately and make them jig and jag as real Zeros do, trying to avoid the lethal hail. So there was Eberhart—that supposedly tender, poetical soul whom his friends predicted might lose his muse in the war—there was Eberhart reveling in the heart-pounding clatter of the machine guns, the rain of hot brass, and the success of another Zero crashing into the sea!

Was this activity the end of Dad's muse? In later years, I'd hear Allen Ginsberg opine that the single greatest English language poem ever to come out of World War II is Dad's "The Fury of Aerial Bombardment." Probably Dad wrote its first three stanzas in his heart while he jigged and jagged the kite, and the bullets howled over his head. What makes that poem great is the sharp transition to its fourth and last stanza. Dad told me that he waited several days before he added those precise, stark words of the fourth stanza that name the dead and leave us readers with that shiver of awe . . . and of truth.

No, the call of the muse upon my father was always strong.

By 1946, my father was busy demobilizing navy airmen as they streamed home through the Golden Gate, away from places whose names are seared into the American soul—from Midway, from Guadalcanal, from Leyte Gulf, from Iwo Jima, from Okinawa—and most especially away from the buildup for the final invasion of the Japanese home islands. Thank God, as Dad used to remark to me—but sotto voce, because after the late 1960s it was incorrect to say this sort of thing out loud—thank God for Little Boy. Little Boy was the name of the atomic bomb that we dropped on Hiroshima, thus forcing five years of slaughter to come to an end.

While my father was busy on the base, my mother was busy noticing something else. Babies!

There were lots of sailors back home from the sea, and everywhere Mom looked there were babies. My mother told me that she and Dad had never done anything to prevent babies, but for four years of war no baby had occurred. So there they were in the spring of 1946, and the war was over, and soon enough my father himself would be demobilized, and there would be ordinary life to pursue. (He was due to be promoted to captain, but in the end, he left the navy two months before he achieved that rank.)

Of course, as I have said, Dad was a poet even when he was a machine-gun trainer, and he struck up friendships with poets wherever he went. One San Francisco friendship was with Kenneth and Marie Rexroth. Kenneth was to become a central figure after the war in what has been called the "San Francisco Renaissance," which helped to launch, among other things, the Beat poets.

One day, Dad and Mom were invited to a party at the Rexroths' apartment. The two couples had not met. Dad dressed formally, in a white uniform, resplendent with gold braid. He and Mom knocked and were bidden to enter.

Gasps.

Stricken silence.

Who were these . . . military people?

This couldn't be Eberhart.

Not Eberhart of "The Groundhog." Not the Eberhart who wrote "If I Could Only Live at the Pitch That Is Near Madness."

But of course it was that Eberhart, and the crowd was charmed, and Dad and Mom remained close friends with Kenneth and Marie from then on, even after the Rexroths' 1948 split, with equal affection for them both.

A little more than twenty years later, I was part of a reunion between Dad, Mom, and Marie at her forest-shaded, very California house on a slope north of San Francisco Bay. "So this is the very boy," Marie said when I was introduced. "Ha-ha!"

I didn't get her meaning until later, though I enjoyed her company.

The point of this Rexroth story, though, is that sometime in February 1946, Kenneth and Marie, and Dad and Mom, went off for a weekend drive north of San Francisco to the tiny town of Inverness, which is located on a spit of water that nearly separates the mainland from the wonderful wildness (or so it was then) of Point Reyes.

During the drive, Marie happened to spot some newly born lambs in a pasture, and she and my mother begged the men to stop the car so they could enjoy a brief time gamboling with— or maybe just looking at—the lambs. Back in the car, the two couples proceeded to Inverness and there took rooms for the night at a local inn. My mother liked to tell me it must have been the lambs. Or if she were in less febrile a mood, she'd surmise that maybe they were all just relaxed at the end of the war. Maybe it was the good company and some wonderful conversation, she said. But anyway, next morning, there was something different going on in the Eberhart household, and that difference was me.

* * *

Most days of my life began with Dad rubbing my head to wake me from sleep and ended with him removing his pipe to kiss me good night. Mine was, in truth, a blessed life.

But I was angry, ten or fifteen years after my initial appearance on the scene. I loved my parents, and I loved my sister, Gretchen, when she came along about five years after I did. I loved art, too. But art, I soon discovered, can eat you for lunch.

PART TWO

I walked through the church's door and sat in the rear-most pew. Shortly, the pastor asked us to stand and to sing a hymn.

There I stood, a Jew, in the back pew of Small Point Baptist Church, surrounded by strangers. We had finished two hymns, and instead of asking us to sit down and to listen to his sermon, Pastor Dan Coffin had instructed us to turn around and to greet one another . . . particularly, he contin-ued, "If you see someone you don't know, greet that person."

Oh, darn.

Dutifully, I stepped from my pew and held out my hand to the man in the pew before me. He took my hand in two of his, looked me deeply in the eye, and said, "How nice it is to have you here."

I was confused. He didn't know me.

All around me, people had debouched from their pews and jammed the aisles, hugging one another, shaking hands, kissing, laughing.

It went on and on. By the time Pastor Dan waved us back to attention, seven or eight minutes had passed, and I was ten pews away from my seat. I'd been greeted, truly hailed, by twenty people, each equally delighted to have me here at church with them. I'd begun to respond with my own greeting back, as though I knew them—though I did not. This was cordiality of a quality I had never experienced before in a holy setting. It was beyond mere amiability. Something else was active here; something else was walking in these aisles.

Next in the service came prayer requests. This person had decided finally to have the operation, and it was scheduled for next week. That person was traveling to see grandchildren. One man, tearfully, thanked the congregation for its prayers for his son, an army rifleman deployed in Iraq. For ten minutes, we discussed the medical and emotional urgencies of the congregation.

This, too, was new to me. Who were these people that they should so commonly share these intimate details?

Pastor Dan then delivered a thirty-minute message that was intelligent, direct, biblical, and plain, before ending the service with the exhortation, "Have a great week in the Lord!"

Before the service began, Pastor Dan had invited any visitors to fill out a card. This I never do. However, after the service, I got one of the cards and filled it out. Then, instead of slinking out the door—this I always do—I approached him, handed him my visitor card, and introduced myself. We had a vigorous conversation of ten minutes before I hurried home with an excited report for Channa.

She and I were thrilled. So I called the pastor, feeling diffident to interrupt his Sunday afternoon, yet urgent to hear more from him. We made a date for him to visit our home.

I assumed it would be a visit of half an hour, for a cup of tea and a cookie, and I assumed it would have a cool New England austerity about it. Not so. Three hours after Pastor Dan sat down on our couch, he had elicited the details of both Channa's and my spiritual journeys. And he had offered a first answer to my plaint.

"But still I don't get it about Jesus."

"Jesus," he said, "is the love in the fellowship."

"Oh!"

I said no more. But I made what was the beginning of a connection. That's who had been passing among the pews.

Goodness.

What a predicament.

CHAPTER SEVEN

"But you said!"

"I said what?"

"You said she'd be here."

"She is here, you rude boy. Now come downstairs this min-ute and be polite."

"It's not her."

"Of course it's she, Dikkon. Who else could she be?"

"She's just a woman," I wailed, a six-year-old deprived of his dream.

Mom sat down on my bed and laughed. "Oh, you poor boy. I'm so sorry. I understand what you must have thought. But she's a nice woman, and she's a friend of mine, and I want you to come downstairs right now and politely say hello, and then I'll ask her to laugh like the Wicked Witch of the West, and then you'll see."

So I did go downstairs, and Margaret Hamilton *did* laugh like the Wicked Witch of the West, and she *was* a nice woman, but whenever I saw her later I understood her to be another of those people who flocked to my parents' cordiality and who were not quite what they seemed. I had become accustomed to people who were not quite what they seemed. I assumed that not-quite-seeming should be my own stance too, when I grew bigger and when I, too, should need to seem.

But as a six-year-old, I was still disappointed that the Wicked Witch of the West had not been in her expected costume when she knocked on our door.

We were living in Cambridge then, on Hilliard Place, and Dad and Mom were having a whirl of a time of it. Dad was selling floor wax for his father-in-law and was covering much of New England. This was great for him because it gave him an excuse to go off and meet other poets.

For example, Dad's friendship with the Pulitzer Prize–winning poet Wallace Stevens began when Dad called on the Hartford and tried to persuade that insurance company to switch to Butcher's wax. Wallace Stevens, ultimately a Hartford vice president, was the man he had to convince. Dad, the younger businessman-poet, may have closed a wax deal with the older businessman-poet's company—I don't know—but Dad always said that their friendship grew because they had *two* languages to speak to one another, not just one, as each of them tangled all day with corporate policy and quotas and wrote hard at night to restore their souls.

Dad's increasing fame provided him with endless opportunities to mingle with East Coast artists and writers. Art was bursting out all over, now that the war was done, and Dad and Mom were in the thick of it.

My fame was bursting out all over too. Everything about my

life seemed important to me, and I had many tales to tell my small classmates at Shady Hill School. One of the best of my tales was the one about my mother and Hitler. You already know what actually happened at their meeting, but here's how I had heard of it from Mom—I swear. I swear that Mom told me that when she was young in Germany before the war, she and Hitler had *danced* together.

And why not? Wasn't my mother beautiful? And wasn't Hitler's a famous name—for some reason or other that I did not know? Indeed, it was quite easy for me to see my beautiful mother dancing finely with the elegant Hitler. In my head, theirs was a Rogers-and-Astaire moment, both of them stylishly slim, with "The Blue Danube" playing in the background and my mother following every move of the graceful Hitler, only backwards—as the real Ginger Rogers pointed out that she must do—and in high heels.

So that's how I told the tale to my pals. It worked, just as I planned. I basked in the fame of my mother. The tale impressed them to no end. The tale also impressed the school administration and the parents of all the other children to no end, when they heard about it. Then erupted the sort of brouhaha that appealed to my mother's sense of humor very much. Just imagine what those other people had been thinking of her! And just imagine what a great laugh they were all to have when it was finally straightened out!

*　　*　　*

In Cambridge, I used to sit halfway down the stairs (that was the rule: no farther) and listen intently to the grown-up talk in the living room. All the writers passing to and fro, talking,

talking, talking. The smoke was thick; the air was alive with words. There were shouts of laughter; there was the clink of ice.

These were the people, it seemed to me—though of course I had not yet read "Prufrock" as a six-year-old and would not have used such a metaphor as this—these were the people who dared to eat *all* the peaches.

Eventually, Jeanie, our upstairs boarder—part of whose rent was babysitting for me—would come up from the party and shoo me to bed. Even in bed I could still hear it sometimes— the talk, the endless, striving, and important talk. Mom would come and kiss me. Now and then, one of the poets would put his or her head in the door and wish me well. We were connected, they and I. There were some of them—Richard "Dick" Wilbur especially, and his wife, Charlotte, and also Dylan Thomas—who made time for me.

Dylan used to read bedtime stories to me. I realize now that he was probably drunk, but there were times when he wanted to escape from the party, and he would come and sit by my bed and read to me. I remember him as having a chubby face and wild hair, and I believe I remember his amusing accent, though that memory could be influenced by later hearings of his recorded voice doing *A Child's Christmas in Wales*.

Later I learned that quite often when Dylan came upstairs he had just made a pass at my mother. Mom rejected him enough that eventually he stopped. But she told me that she took his attentions mostly as braggadocio. If she'd said, "Okay, Dylan, this is a good time, let's go upstairs right now," she believed he would have backed out. Dylan had his image as the brash bohemian to maintain, and of course, Caitlin, his wife, was safely tucked away back in Ireland. Mom believed Dylan liked to give himself credit for affronting traditional principles when he propositioned her, yet he could do so safely because she always said no.

On the many party nights, if I were lonely up in my bed, I could desire a glass of water. That was permissible. The best water in our house, of course, came from downstairs, from the kitchen tap. I drank a lot of downstairs water on party nights.

If I should call down to Mom and say that I was really, really thirsty, I'd be allowed to come downstairs for a few minutes. Then, cunningly, I would linger, glass in hand. Usually I could make one last ceremonial round of the habitués, and I would be patted and toasted. I learned from my father to hold my glass up high and to clink. Always on the center of the table was the Golden Rose of the New England Poetry Club, which my father had been awarded, and from whose petals, or so it seemed to me, rays of light spangled the laughing crowd, reflecting off their eyes and their highballs and their wits. I raised my water glass to be one of them—hurrah!

Actually what I was quaffing was the liquid I truly desired: the wine of poetic vintage that intoxicated me then and makes me merry still.

*   *   *

Dad knew almost all of the writers and poets on the East Coast, and his ability to connect with people made him a natural choice when the *New York Times* wanted to send someone to the West Coast to scope out the poetry scene there. After all, Dad already knew most of the Beats out west from his war years.

During the war years, many Beats established their leftist chops. To leftist critics then, after the war the Beats were honeypots: their antiestablishment rhetoric was nectar. Many of the Beats clustered around San Francisco—Kenneth Rexroth (though I've heard him argue that he was not himself a Beat) and many others who experimented with the artistic ecstasy and the artistic possibility of drunkenness, or of madness. They steeped themselves in esoteric symbolism, Eastern religion, automatic writing, and dream sequence. They explored the outer fringes of sex, of marriage, of family relationships.

So here came my bright-eyed dad—himself a leader of the eastern literary establishment, now a poet who wore a suit to work, who sat on corporate boards, who married only one woman and stayed married to her for fifty-two years—here came my dad to hang with the crowd that would later establish City Lights Books in 1953 and to report back to easterners what that crowd had to say for itself.

City Lights was the first all-paperback bookstore in the United States, and it was also a publisher. Poet Lawrence Ferlinghetti started the store—and later, when I was in college, took the time to instruct me how to use a stage microphone, at which he was masterful—and the store was the publisher of Allen Ginsberg's breakout poem "Howl." Dad thought that "Howl" was "a magnificent new *Leaves of Grass*" with which to shock the stiff attitudes of his newspaper readers back in Manhattan.

Allen had been urged by his therapist to break away from traditional verse forms and by Rexroth to break away from stilted language and to use his own raw voice. So in "Howl," Allen employed line forms and breath pacing that others among the Beats would later adopt. In 1956, US Customs confiscated City Lights's edition of *Howl and Other Poems* and arrested Larry

Ferlinghetti for obscenity. The 1957 trial, which Ferlinghetti won, became an important First Amendment decision.

Dad loved the Beats. Particularly he loved them for their artistic energy and for the hot enthusiasm of their imaginations. He told the Easterners about this in crisp *New York Times* prose; that was his assignment. On the other hand, Dad was leery of the Beat lifestyle. Nor was Dad as hungry for popular media notice as, particularly, was Ginsberg.

Ginsberg was a master at attracting publicity. For example, during the Vietnam War he made himself media candy with his bongo, cymbal, and chanting appearances in San Francisco's Golden Gate Park as he protested the war. It was amusing for me to see Allen on TV making himself a symbol for the hippies. I knew him well enough by then to see that it was really just Allen himself after all, there on the TV. The real Allen was a middle-aged, homosexual, Jewish Beat poet, born in Newark, NJ, who was stylishly Buddhist in the 1960s (and perhaps deeply and theologically Buddhist as well—how can one tell about another man's heart?), and he didn't wear shoes.

I had always liked Ginsberg. He could be funny, and in any event he *looked* funny during that time in the late 1960s, dressed as he was in his white, flowing robes as though he were some Eastern mystic—although at the same time he wore a thick, black, Amish-preacher beard. There were times, though, when Allen's sense of humor got buried by his urgency to make a scene. Such was the case on one of Allen's visits to us in Hanover, New Hampshire, when Dad was poet in residence and professor of English at Dartmouth.

The day Allen arrived in Hanover, he and Peter Orlovsky, who was his partner, and several Hanoverians who loved the idea of having Allen—*Allen!*—among them descended upon the very conventional Hanover Inn to register. The fact that Allen was not wearing shoes put up the backs of the innkeepers, and Allen was refused a room. This infuriated Allen, and he fumed all the way to our house. He continued to fulminate against all small-minded, stiff-necked, straitlaced, hidebound Victorian innkeepers until Mom, ever the practical one, tired of it and said, "But, Allen, why not just put on a pair of shoes to register and then take them off afterward?"

No! That would never do. Allen needed to make a scene. But by that time—and with Mom's twinkle to assist—he had begun to see the humor in the situation after all, and then we had supper.

The next morning we were sitting around the kitchen, talking wars, then and now. War was Allen's vocation of the moment. He had always been opposed to what he took to be his nation's militarism, as well as opposed to its sexual repression, its capitalist economics, and now especially its prejudice against those who do not wear shoes.

Earlier I mentioned that Allen felt, categorically, that Dad's "Fury of Aerial Bombardment" was the greatest poem to come out of World War II. He was right: the poem is great. But I was also aware that his use of Dad's poem was self-serving. Allen was reading the poem not to celebrate its literary greatness but rather to support his own antiwar stance. Dad had not written the poem to support that perspective. Dad was simply the machine-gun officer who reveled in the rain of hot brass yet who cried upon God to explain it all, even so.

This example of the use by critics of art for their own purpose, and not for the author's intended purpose, underscores a message my father often gave to me. This message was central to his wisdom. "No, Dikkon," he would say to me. "I can't control what they say, the critics. They say what they say for their reasons, not for mine." Then he would puff a philosophical puff or two and conclude, "Dikkon, the truth is, once you publish a poem, it doesn't belong to you anymore."

There were many times when I was young that I wished Dad would apply that very apt wisdom to the "publishing" and then to the raising of his own son.

CHAPTER EIGHT

When I was in second grade, we lived in Storrs, Connecticut. Dad had his usual post at the University of Connecticut as poet in residence, a one-year stint. Gretchen was two; I was seven. We lived in a two-story building comprising two faculty apartments, one of four such buildings in a quadrangle. It was winter. Gretchen's and my bedrooms were on our second floor.

As happened regularly, one night I was awakened by Gretchen crying from her bedroom. I knew the routine: she'd cry for a little while, and then Dad or Mom—usually Mom— would come upstairs. I'd hear murmuring, and in a minute or two Gretchen would be quiet. Usually Mom would look in on me afterward, and I'd get a kiss. All very comfy. This time, though, Gretchen kept crying, and no one came up.

I remember waiting, drifting in and out of sleep, but growing increasingly puzzled that no one came up. What was wrong? Eventually I was sufficiently wide awake to feel annoyed. Gretchen was keeping me awake. She needed to be changed. Where was Mom? I got out of bed. I went into Gretchen's room to see if perhaps Mom might already be there. But no Mom. I decided to go and get Mom myself.

Why Mom hadn't heard Gretchen crying was a mystery. Ours was not a big apartment, and the sound of her crying ought to have carried everywhere. When I descended our stairs, I emerged into the living room and dining room. The apartment had an open-concept design. Everywhere in the downstairs, kitchen included, was visible from the base of the stairs. I remember standing there, puzzled. No Mom. No Dad. I wasn't alarmed yet, but this was odd.

First of all, something needed to be done—right now—to make Gretchen stop. God must have designed the crying of a baby for that very purpose.

I knew all about changing diapers. One of the conversations I had had with my parents when we discussed my about-to-arrive sibling had to do with how I could help with what they told me was going to be a very happy but busy time. My idea was that I could be in charge of the rubber pants.

In later years, my mother would recall this choice of mine and wonder how that idea had sprung so fully formed into my head. (Sometimes she recalled this publicly, with embarrassing effect when I was, say, twelve.) But rubber pants were indeed my job, and I took them seriously. I hung them up to dry when they had been washed, I folded them when they were dry, and I stored them in their proper spot on the bassinet. And I was in charge of getting them onto Gretchen's legs after the actual diaper business was complete.

I went back upstairs. I got Gretchen out of bed and onto the bassinet. I took off her pajamas, removed the old diaper, put on a new one (as far as I know, without sticking her with a pin), and then realized that I couldn't just put her back into pajamas. We were in the middle of an emergency. It was a quiet emergency to be sure—the house wasn't burning down—but there were no grown-ups. They had simply vanished. I wasn't quite certain what to do, but I knew that whatever I did, it would be better if Gretchen were dressed. So I dressed her.

I didn't dress myself. It must have been at this point that I began to have an idea of what to do. I would take Gretchen next door, and our friends, the grown-ups in the next apartment, would look after her while I tried to figure out what had become of our parents.

So Gretchen and I walked downstairs to the front door. I remember getting her into all the covering she might need outside—boots, scarf, coat, mittens, and hat. For my sister, this was an interesting adventure in the middle of the night, and she was having fun. I was not having fun. I was trying to think out the necessary steps, in their proper order, to save my sister, but I was frightened as well. What if the grown-ups had vanished from next door, too? Then what was I to do? What if there were no grown-ups anywhere anymore? As a second grader, I had no concept of the Rapture, but I was as disoriented as though the Rapture had occurred, and Gretchen and I had been left behind.

However, first things first: throw my jacket over my pajamas to keep the snow off. Gretchen must be protected from all dangers; I just needed to stay dry.

It was snowing that night.

I opened our door and pushed outside into the cold and the snow. Holding Gretchen's hand, I led her down our pathway to the curb of the street, turned left, walked to the next shoveled pathway, and walked up to the next apartment's front door. We climbed a few steps and stood on the stoop. I rang the bell. I remember hoping fervently that there might be grown-ups in this apartment.

There were grown-ups!

"May we come in? We have no mother."

Ever afterward, the description of us two little kids in the middle of the night, standing on the stoop in the snow, made a famous tale. Oh, the cuteness of it!

And, oh, the chagrin of my parents. They were in another of the apartments, probably no more than one hundred yards away, playing bridge.

How I was praised—for my maturity in a crisis, and for my wisdom, and for how carefully I had dressed my sister! How often I heard the funny story of how Mom or Dad had frequently returned from the bridge game—whoever was dummy—and had checked on us throughout the evening.

But not that one time! Wouldn't you just know!

Looking back on this event as an adult, I can understand the cute side of it, and I remember being pleased that I was thought to have been mature. But I also remember being confused about how easily the event—which had frightened me—was turned into a tale to amuse dinner guests and others. I received additional compliments from those guests—again, how mature. But this was an early experience of what was a theme in my family's life: the overshadowing of the reality by the created story.

Those who have lived in an artistic family may have experienced the same thing. In fact, those who have lived in a family dominated by any force larger than itself probably have experienced the same thing. As a child, I loved the fact that our family was different—Grandmother's five names, Mom's "dance" with Hitler, the admiration from Dad's fans who would stop him on the street and speak passionately about his, or their, verses. For me as an impressionable child, though, there was another side of it.

As a seven- or eight-year-old, I experienced fright. But I was not allowed to keep it for my discharge of it. I learned that the correct thing to do with my emotion was to give it up to my parents, to be used for their charm. At my young age, I adored my parents, and I knew the story was funny . . . since it had come out all right. But what if it had not? What would we be saying then?

I love stories—I write them, I act them, I sell them. For many, many years I assumed I could live them. In fact, I did live them—or tried to.

It took this son of the poet way too long to begin to understand what facts are. We're callow, we Eberhart artist types. We truly believe we can make the world adjust to our story, and not the other way around.

Here's another iteration. Once, Gretchen almost drowned. I saved her. Again, my feeling afterward was confusion.

Here is the scene.

We were at our family's summer cottage in Maine. Rocky beach. Evening. Low tide. Gretchen was about five. I was about ten. Gretchen could not swim. Everyone—dozens of friends and relatives—was up at the top of the beach where one of the famous clambakes was steaming. Cocktails on the rocks. (Get it: on the rocks, ha-ha.)

General jollity.

Gretchen and I were playing in the ocean. Not big waves;

about average. We'd found a big drift log, and it was our toy. It was big enough so we could sit astride it, and it would still float. Gretchen wanted to try. I was out of the water by then, walking up the beach. Mom had been by the water a moment before. As I walked, I saw Gretchen from the corner of my eye sitting on the log. The next time I glanced, she was off the log. I couldn't see her head. She must be on the other side of the log from my view.

In another second, I'll see her. I stopped and watched.

I didn't see her.

I remember streaking down the beach and into the water. Gretchen was tangled up underneath the log. She was thrashing wildly, already partly full of water, mouth open, eyes wide, frantic. I remember pulling at her and trying to shove the stupid log out of the way. It was very awkward, and everything was going very slowly. Finally I got her yanked out of the water, face up, and I remember her terrified look. I hauled her ashore, too frightened myself to shout. I rolled her onto her stomach and tried to empty her out.

A moment later, there were people running. Now everything would be all right, and it was. Probably the entire incident took less than a minute. But in another minute or three, Gretchen might have been dead. And I had only just happened to look. A parent's worst nightmare had swept across the beach, only to be diverted in its wild career by the happenstance of my turning my head.

Again, I was praised. Again, I didn't want the praise. What I wanted was for scary things not to happen to Gretchen and me, whose grandmother had five names, and whose mother danced with Hitler, and whose father was admired by people we didn't even know.

Years later, Dad took me to meet E. E. Cummings at Cummings's farm in New Hampshire. I was in prep school, and I thought "in Just-" and "Buffalo Bill's" were wonderful and "she being Brand" was the sexiest thing I had ever read (far sexier, really, than the carefully underlined sections of *Peyton Place* my pal Steve lent me for late-night reading).

As we were driving over, I learned from Dad that when Cummings was young, he saved his sister from drowning. What happened was this. Cummings and his sister and their dog were in a canoe that capsized. The dog panicked and tried to climb on top of the sister. In order to save his sister, Cummings had been forced to drown his dog.

When Dad told me about this incident, I remember how mythic it seemed to him and with what a trembling voice he told of it: it was a tale of such elementals as almost to have sprung among the demigods, or so Dad's demeanor indicated.

Here was Dad, singing rhapsodically about another member of his club, and I had done the very same thing! Why was he not at that moment rhapsodizing about me?

But I knew Dad, and here is how I understood the difference between the two incidents. Gretchen and I were just Gretchen and I. We were part of the weft and warp of his life, and the saving of Gretchen by me was merely an incident among a thousand other incidents; no poetry there. But that other incident— now, that was something fine. Boy Loves Dog (that's elemental). Boy Drowns Dog to Save Sister, whom he also Loves (another elemental). Heroic Boy and Sister Survive (better and better). Boy Left to Muse on Death and Life (bingo: a poem!).

CHAPTER NINE

Dad left the Butcher Polish Company when he was invited
to spend a year at the University of Washington as its visiting
poet in residence. Dad's pal Robert Frost had invented the job
of "barding around the country"—moving from one post or
appointment to the next—and Dad wanted in. So from 1952
onward, we followed Dad as he "barded around" to various universities. What was important to me was that each summer, our
family returned to Undercliff, our Maine cottage at the eastern
end of a long, rocky beach at the head of a wide cove (and the
scene of Gretchen's near drowning).

Ah, Undercliff!

Heaven on earth.

The cottage looks south, through a scrim of islands and out to
sea. Our view is of East Penobscot Bay, noted by many yachtsmen
as one of the finest cruising archipelagos in the world. There are
five cottages backing that beach or in the woods behind the beach,
and there is a larger dwelling farther inland, a farm. Collectively,
the beach, the cottages, the farm, and the land around them are
named Undercliff.

This is because Undercliff's eastern boundary is a very steep rise of land—to about one hundred feet—with sheer granite faces. Since our cottage is the easternmost cottage, ours is close under the actual cliff. The height of the cliff blocks the early sun from coming in, so our cottage is not good for you if you depend on sunrises to glorify your day. However, if you are a person who likes to linger over talk and drinks into the evening—as a sunset builds, crests, and dissolves to your west like a painting by Frederic Edwin Church—then our cottage is a very fine place indeed.

Our Undercliff cottage was the only one among the five cottages that was privately owned; the other cottages were summer rentals owned by the family that, in those early days, occupied the farm. Ours was a red, two-story, uninsulated Cape Cod, built for summer use on a foundation of loose stone and brick rubble, with a central chimney, three bedrooms, and for many years—but no longer—a back ell, which was used as an extra visitors' bunkroom.

We needed that extra visitors' bunkroom because when I say that Undercliff was the summer cottage for our family, I do not mean just for Dad, Mom, Gretchen, and me.

Each summer, our cottage was flooded with uncles and aunts, cousins and friends, many of the friends being of such intimacy as, really, to be family themselves. Indeed, there was scarcely room left over for our *other* family—that is, for the poets and for their associated spouses, children, lovers, dogs, and manuscripts. Our parents were fervent in their perpetual invitations to all: "This summer, you *must* come see us in Maine!"

They came, indeed. They came, and they came, and they came. When Gretchen and I were old enough to be reflective about this poetic inundation, our eyes would roll at one another. Should we run such a summer circus, if we were in charge? Not hardly.

"You *must* come see us in Maine!"

What an invitation! Who would decline such a plea? Who would skip the gathering of poets—salted with plain, regular folks—brought together by ebullient Dick and Betty Eberhart, anytime between June and September, on our conglomerate shore, often with lobsters thrown in?

In summer, back then as well as now, the population of Maine explodes with visitors seeking what our family had already. Sometimes the visitors are successful in their search, sometimes unsuccessful. They might be waylaid by shopping centers or by ersatz "real-Maine" entertainments, or they might be funneled straight to Bar Harbor, where they take a spin and then return from whence they came. What they want to find, instead, is a little nook by the ocean, plain and simple, where their world might slow down for a bit or where they might find enchantment.

When I was young, I experienced our happy summers without being aware of how idyllic they were when compared with a lot of the world's less halcyon experiences.

Here's an example of what those travelers sought to experience. This is the sort of magical, poetical event that might beguile you when you first explored "down east," as the Maine shoreline is called—or anytime, for that matter, when you spent time around Dad.

Once, many years ago, poet Daniel Hoffman and his wife, Liz—incidentally, Liz was the poetry editor of the *Ladies' Home Journal* during the twelve years when that magazine published verse—Dan and Liz were driving in a leisurely manner along the Maine shoreline, following the fingers and bays, no particular destination, just driving and looking, enjoying Maine for the first time. Dan, a poet of precise craftsmanship and deliberation as well as an essayist, and later a United States Poet Laureate, was about twenty years younger than my father and was at that time a great admirer of Dad's work, though he had never met Dad, nor had he any particular knowledge of where Dad lived.

So that day, Dan and Liz were meandering along a back road, and they chanced upon a dirt lane to their left, which they surmised might bring them close to the sea. Should they take it? Why not? So they turned down that lane—picturesque in itself—and rambled along. By and by, they saw that the lane did indeed lead them to a beach. There was no one around, so they parked their car in a field by the top of the beach and went and sat on a great mass of driftwood at the tide line and watched the ocean. It was a sunny, warm day in summer, they were far away from home, they were in love, and this was all so charmingly rustic, all around.

After some time had passed, they noticed out to sea an outboard motorboat that seemed to be moving in their direction, perhaps from three or four miles away, tiny in the distance. They watched it idly. In time, their idleness dissipated as they focused more intently on the boat, which interestingly enough was still on a direct approach to their area. Time passed, and the boat grew closer, and they could see more detail. They saw that there was a burly man standing in the boat's stern, with his hand on the motor's tiller, and on her steeply raised bow there was—was it a dog?—yes, it was a dog hanging over her prow.

Curiously, the boat continued toward them, toward their

very beach, and—yes—*directly* toward them, where they sat at the top of that beach, at its western end, with the tide at half. The boat never wavered one inch in its approach. Now Dan and Liz were riveted to it.

The boat's approach was so precisely toward them that there was an eerie quality about the moment, as though the world were holding its breath before some revelation should occur. Now the boat was in their cove. Still it wavered not one inch. Shortly, the man driving the boat slowed his engine, killed it, and bent to tip its propeller up out of the water. The boat crunched ashore. The dog jumped off the prow and loped up the beach toward Dan and Liz, wagging. The man clambered forward across the thwarts, stepped ashore, and came up the beach after the dog.

Dan stood, not knowing what was to occur.

The man was hearty, broad, having a brown Lincoln beard spotted with grey. He stuck out his hand. "Hello! I'm Richard Eberhart. Who are you?"

Dan loves to recall this moment, of this mariner come out of the sea, one of his favorite poet voices, arrowing as though magically toward him and Liz, where they had chanced to sit that day—without knowing it—on Undercliff's beach.

Some years later, Dan and Liz bought the old farm above Bakeman's Beach, just down the road, and they became frequent "family" at Undercliff and out on the bay aboard Dad's cabin cruiser, *Reve*.

Reve was magnificent. One year when I was about ten, Dad had some poetry money in his pocket, and he wanted a bigger boat. He found *Reve* tied to a dock in Bar Harbor. She had been meticulously restored by a couple of guys who wanted $5,000 for her. Dad offered $3,000; they said no; he walked away. He told me afterward that he spent the next week in agonies of worry before returning to the dock to see her still tied there. He made his $3,000 offer once again. It was late in the season. To the restorers who wanted $5,000, getting 60 percent was better than getting nothing, especially as they would need to haul her out of the water and store her through another winter.

The deal was made.

So Dad; Hal Vaughan, who owned our local boatyard; neighbor and poet Philip Booth; another neighbor, Robert Lowell, fondly known as "Cal"; and I went the next day back to Bar Harbor and brought *Reve* home, which was a day's steaming from Frenchman Bay to Penobscot Bay. We brought her home, where she would reside for the next thirty years as the focus of many a summer extravaganza, and where she was dubbed "The *African Queen* of Penobscot Bay" by Elizabeth Hardwick, Cal's wife, because of the funny way that Dad now and then needed to jump around and bang on this or that to keep her going.

Built in 1926 by Consolidated Shipbuilding of New York, *Reve* was thirty-six feet of pure perfection. She slept four below (until we removed her pipe berths; then she slept two), and at that time she was still powered by an old Gray Marine Straight Six engine. Best of all for us kids, she had a cockpit at her bow, where you could tend to the anchor, haul up the mooring buoy, or—if you were the son of her captain—stand in the fog and call back directions to her skipper about how to avoid the lobster-pot buoys.

I reflect on Undercliff's attraction to the poets who made their ways to our door—or who found themselves there anyway, without trying, as Dan and Liz did. Of course, Dad and Mom were the principal attraction. The gatherings that were held each evening, for talk and more talk—as though my parents ran a daily salon—these were gatherings that included nonpoets and nonwriters and nonartists, too. The varied company may have been a relaxing change for the poets. Usually they vied against their scrapping competitors for page space and fellowships and editorial access and reviewer attention, and gossiped about who was doing what to whom.

At Undercliff, instead, they could relax. They could hear what a priest or a lawyer or a government type might have to say on the subject, whatever the subject might happen to be. Even better, they might hear what a lobsterman or a boatbuilder or a goat farmer or a copper miner or a roofer or a back-to-the-lander might have to say on the subject—authentic stuff!

Mom's family had vacationed within a few miles of Under-cliff since 1910. One of the attractions of the whole area was the farm. There I spent time assisting with haying, helping to groom and muck out after the horses, learning to milk by hand and to care for the calves. These were happy activities for me when there was too much wind or fog to sail or when I was mad at my parents.

The family that owned the rest of Undercliff had three chil-dren; their middle child and oldest daughter was my own age. Jenny was my bosom buddy during our summers before puberty. I might complain to her about my parents, and she would abso-lutely definitely complain to me about hers, as we saddled horses from Jenny's family farm and rode off. She and I had a secret spot under an enormous pine blowdown at the top of the cliff. Some of our best times were held right there, and no one knew where we were—no parent, that is.

Jenny's and my life together was great.

Until it got bad.

It was great until my bosom buddy arrived one summer accompanied by a bosom of a different type entirely. Electrified by Jenny's other sort of bosom, I was at the same time befuddled. For years, we had wrestled. How could I wrestle with her any longer? Just what do you *do* with a bosom buddy with a bosom? And already intimidated, I was floored by Jenny's first gushing question to me: "Dikkon, don't you just love progressive jazz?" That did it. I was pretty sure I knew what jazz was—it's music, isn't it?—but *progressive* jazz? Are we *supposed* to love it?

That summer I spent more time building a model of a clipper ship than scrambling up the cliff with Jenny to our secret place.

But always I reveled in the very heat of summer. Now was the hay time—sweet, hot, hay time—with scythe-sharp slither through white, dry hay. We helped at another neighboring farm. With tired arms and shoulders and with itchy, prickly legs, at midday we ate small meat pies still hot from the wood oven while we lounged in the shade of the hay wagon, and we drank an old-time molasses cooler that was admired by my mother but was not nearly as good as orange pop.

The farm sons watched me suspiciously, and I watched them, too. We kept our distance, though Mom wanted me to be friendly. The sons were better with farm tools than I was; I was inept. At night, though, when I opened *Beowulf* to my last-night's page (each summer I reread that formative tale, seeking to get back to the very base of our human story, to our human story of heroes and demons), I suspected that the farm sons were not doing the same.

Despite my confusion about how to satisfy Mom's desire that I be friends with the farm sons, the world was grand indeed. Lilacs still snapped purple each year in a hot May wind. The days were a long slide of happiness broken only by rainstorms and fog. Now came raspberries and blackberries, and mackerel ran in the coves. It was July—lilies and lupine and all the way through to the daisies. The iodine smell of hot rockweed blew in from the beach. The wind picked up, and it was blueberries—August and heavier waves crashed the shore.

Mom and Gretchen and I weeded the roses while bees bumbled drunkenly in a surplus of their pollen. I raced my chartered Dark Harbor 17 in the Saturday Series of the Bucks Harbor Yacht Club, and for two years running, I won the August Cup and was accorded our fleet's best windward skipper—but I often lost when racing leeward, and I often lost to Sal McCloskey (a *girl*!).

Sal McCloskey's father was Robert McCloskey, who wrote and illustrated children's books, the most famous of which is *Make Way for Ducklings*. The McCloskey family summered on an island just across the bay from Undercliff. If you have read the book *One Morning in Maine*—still in print after all these years—you've seen an accurate rendering in Bob's drawings of how the bay looks—where Sal and I and other racers competed with our sloops—and also what the village of South Brooksville looked like in those days (although Bob's drawing takes liberties with the location of the walk up from the harbor). Ferd Clifford, who is shown in the book relaxing in Russell Condon's store, was the man who looked after our cottage when we were away and who took care of the smaller of our boats.

Reve, of course, was the center of it all.

An Undercliff morning would find Mom, with coffee and cigarette, writing one of her millions of letters to a niece, a class-mate, a poet, a poet's wife, a devilish Republican congressman, a dear Democratic congressman, or just a friend from back in the day. Woe to anyone who spoke to her before eleven. Dad would be upstairs in the back bedroom, which was his summer office, banging out another poem on his old Royal typewriter. Then he would be off to the tiny post office in Harborside to mail it to some editor or other. Often Gretchen went with him.

Upon his return came the great question—"Where shall we go in *Reve* today?"

Complicated messages would then be issued among the cottages—children as runners—about a possible afternoon pic-nic on Pond Island. The picnic might work out that day, or it might fail. If it failed, Dad and Gretchen and I might take *Reve* to Bucks Harbor to fill up with gas and ice. If it failed, it might fail because Mom had arranged for a half dozen of the kids to come over in the afternoon and paint the house. The Undercliff cottage was red. My mother painted the house each summer— or rather, she managed a painting crew of twelve-year-olds and younger. Each summer she got about an eighth of the house painted. Next summer she would buy a few gallons of red and begin again where she left off. Each red was different than the last red—but, well, taken all in all, it was still red.

I have never known another such woman as my mother. She frequently discovered at three in the afternoon that there would be fifteen people for dinner and nothing in the house except— after a quick inventory—two cans of spaghetti sauce, a brace of zucchini, a partially used package of hot dogs, and a quart of blueberries. Rather more like a General Bradley, calm and systematic, and unlike the excitable Patton, my mother would marshal her forces, sending some of us down to Scott Nearing's garden to fill up a backseat with fresh vegetables, some of us to Bucks Harbor for a couple of pounds of hamburger, if they had any, and, "Oh, Dikkon, get a lot of nonnutritious cereal and cookies that nobody likes."

"What?"

"That way it doesn't get used up so fast."

We would scatter to our chores. Mom would call after us, "And if you see any kids on the beach, send them over, and we'll make something with these blueberries, maybe a pie. And run up and ask at the farm if there's any new cream we can have. And eggs. Get me a dozen eggs or whatever the hens have laid, and—here, take this basket—if the raspberries are still ripe, stop on the way back and get me some to add to the blueberries."

Two hours later (by this time, of course, the fifteen people have become twenty), we would all sit higgledy-piggledy around the dining table and across the living room enjoying hamburger and hot-dog spaghetti sauce with zucchini and carrots on top of flat noodles because Bucks Harbor's market had no spaghetti that day, a huge salad made from Scott's half-bushel-sized lettuces, toast—very important, toast, at Undercliff—and fresh blueberry "jam" because the pie hadn't turned out quite the way it ought to have. All of which was good enough fodder, but Undercliff was not about the food—it was about the talk, the talk, the talk.

Rarely was I interested in a guest's notoriety. I had been surrounded by famous people most of my life. I was interested in them as individuals, not in their celebrity. But there are times when I find myself disappointed that I had not paid enough attention earlier to a moment that would later be exciting to recall.

For example, I once came upon a copy of the bound screenplay for the 1954 movie *On the Waterfront*, which was written by Budd Schulberg. The screenplay was stuffed back among some tired books in the extra guests' bunkroom at Undercliff. When I hauled the screenplay out and dusted it off, I was swept with happy memories of the movie and—vaguely—with the memory of having met Schulberg himself. I was fascinated by Schulberg's warmly written inscription to Dad and Mom: *For Dick and Betty, Our timing is improving! Happy Reunion and onward, with admiration and great affection, Budd.*

Though the inscription is dated 1986, I did not find the piece until after Dad died. There was no one left to ask for more information. So . . . when I was six or eight, in the early 1950s, had Dad and Schulberg talked about the creating of *On the Waterfront*? I loved that movie. And what might they have said to each other?

When I was speculating about this and realizing there is no way to know—like Mom with the cultivated or the natural pearls—I concluded that, at least in this instance, it is more fun not to know. For me, whether Dad was close to Shulberg during the creation of *On the Waterfront* must be left to the memory of Someone with a much longer perspective than mine.

CHAPTER TEN

On a headland just east of Undercliff there is a small woodland chapel that was built years ago by a summering Episcopal priest, Sewell Emerson. To Dad's delight, Sewell was able to report that his father had known poet Emily Dickinson quite well when he was young. Pictures of Dickinson show her as a dour New England spinster, but Sewell told Dad that his father thought Dickinson quite pretty, really, with a lively face. More important, though, in the view of Sewell's father, Emily Dickinson made especially good doughnuts!

The Emerson chapel has wooden benches, a wheezy pump organ, a bell with a rope that trails down, side-hinged windows, and in its apse, a wide, fixed window looking outward to the sea. There our family sat on Sundays, smelling of sun and salt, and we sang "The Navy Hymn." Usually we arrived at chapel by boat, but sometimes, Before Bosom (that is, before Jenny's bosom), she and I would ride over the intervening hills and arrive only just in time. The horses were curious about God.

They would stick their heads in through an open side window and listen to Father Emerson's sermon too.

Our family attended Episcopal services in whatever town we spent the academic year, but the Emerson chapel is the single consecrated location where I experienced closeness to God. Maybe that had to do with the fact that we were always barefoot. Maybe it had to do with the fact that we went most of the time by boat, and for me, any time in a boat under any nautical condition was a glory. Maybe it was the dogs wandering around and the informality they created, particularly Rock, my favorite among our dogs, who had been a gift from E. B. White's boat-building son, Joel, over on Eggemoggin Reach.

But mostly, I think, it was that Dad was relaxed there. He was not on duty at the chapel. Or even if he felt he was on duty some Sunday, he was on duty simply as a poet. He was not on duty at the chapel as the winner of this or that grand prize or other. He was just a guy—who happened to write stuff.

The most he might be asked to do at chapel would be to recite, which was easy enough. He could do that in his sleep. Or maybe he would be moved to write a poem for a chapel occasion. He did that a few years later for Jenny's wedding. That poem for Jenny's wedding concludes with a couplet that has resounded within me at every wedding I have attended since—

It takes so short a time to get married,
We noticed no change in the tide.

To experience my father relaxed in a consecrated setting—this was to experience art and religion as I knew them then. Later, these two grand human motivations and creative energies were to be the programmatic structure of my doctorate. But then—long before it occurred to me to earn a doctorate or even to know what one was—I sat on the bench beside my dad, or behind him if his bench was full, and I could feel the heat of him. I could smell his dried sweat and the sun smell of his skin, all mixed with a whiff of the Noxzema he lathered on his nose and cheekbones to shield his fairness from the nautical sun. He had probably not shaved—he grew a beard most summers "just to see how gray I am getting"—and I would admire the muscles in his brawny forearms, muscles that raised *Reve*'s heavy, navy-style anchor hand over hand.

I sat beside my father, sucking in the memories and memorizing them, drinking his deepest goodness. Next to him was Mom, and if this scene were to show her at her happiest, she would have a passel of kids surrounding her, all jiggling and being shushed and being smiled at and being tickled and then being shushed all over again.

It is the wisdom of the heart that I was absorbing there in that consecrated seaside chapel, there in that home of our greatest Father.

From the instant we are conceived, our parents are teaching us. They are our most intimate guides regarding the fundamentals of life. Some of their teaching goes awry, yes. Some of their actions are painful, yes. But for most of us, during most of the time, our parents fill our hearts with good.

They fill our *hearts*—that's the point. We cannot gain wisdom purely from the head, although secularists think we can. We cannot gain morality purely from the head, although atheists think we can. No, we absorb wisdom and morality into our *hearts* first, from those who embody them for us from our beginnings.

As a teenage son, I looked to my father for clues regarding manliness, but also regarding male responsibility. Some of the clues I received were easy to admire. My father was physically robust in his forties, fifties, and sixties, when I was watching him most closely, and he had the muscle-memory gift that former athletes have. Having not skied, let's say, for a winter, it took him a mere ten minutes to remember how to do it and how to appear graceful while doing it (however oddly he dressed while doing it—with trousers, white shirt, tie, overcoat, and pipe!).

Speaking of physical robustness, Sydney Lea, now the poet laureate of Vermont, tells the following tale. When Dad was in his late seventies and was the poet laureate of New Hampshire, he was invited to come down from New Hampshire to read somewhere in Connecticut. It was winter, and Mom did not want Dad to drive down alone, so she asked Syd if he would accompany Dad. Syd and Dad were friends, and Syd—in his late forties—said sure. It snowed during the drive. Somewhere in Connecticut, Syd pulled off the highway into a rest stop. As their car came to a stop, it skidded, and its right front wheel bumped up, over, and down on the other side of a parking curb, so the car was immobilized, its one wheel useless.

Syd was astonished when Dad said, "Let me see what I can do." Dad exited the car, walked around to its front, examined the situation, squatted down, positioned his hands under the front bumper, and lifted up the front of the car and scuttled it sideways so the tire could drop down onto the road once again.

"Dick! You just lifted up the front of my car!"

Dad stood a bit taller, twitched his shoulders, jiggled his arms, and grinned. "Yes. I guess I did, didn't I?"

As I am sure is already apparent, I judged Dad superbly

powerful in the muse department also. He dominated the environment when it came to the singing of great praises.

If Dad could make perfect literary moments, then so could I. Here's an event that occurred more times than once. If we were aboard *Reve* and were weaving blindly through a heavy fog, it was my job to stand in the forepeak and to call directions back to Dad at the helm, so that he could steer around the lobster pot buoys.

When I called directions in the fog, I liked to use my nautical vocabulary.

"Buoy ahead fifty yards. Come to port a quarter point."

"What?" Dad yelled forward to me.

I raised my voice higher. "I said buoy ahead fifty yards. Come to port a quarter point."

"What's that?" (This from a naval officer and able seaman.)

"Go left!"

But if we were unlucky, this exchange would have taken too long, and we'd ride over the float line of the lobster pot, Dad would not throw the gear into neutral in time, and the line would catch on the propeller and in two seconds become an impacted mess as big as a soccer ball, thus bringing *Reve* to a halt, rolling and helpless on the sea.

So I would need to strip and, holding a knife in my teeth, drop overboard and swim beneath the transom into the green frigidity of the Gulf of Maine. And Dad's knives were never sharp. In the end, I began to carry my own knife for just this service. But I was frustrated: surely my father must know that I couldn't with fewer than four hands—one hand to keep me from being battered by the stern as she pounded, one hand to steady me on the rudder, and one hand to hack away at the pot buoy line. Then, when the tangle began to loosen, another hand to grab the ends, so they would not unravel too fast and slip away, thus robbing the lobsterman not only of his potential catch but of a valuable trap, too.

But of course, my father had been right: I *could* manage the task—with only two hands. Gasping and frozen, and clutching the two cut ends of the pot line, I'd haul myself back aboard, firmly knot the two ends together again, toss the thing over the side, and receive the congratulations of whatever delighted poets were with us on that particular ride.

This was fine manly stuff, but it would not have been needed if Dad had turned a quarter point to port.

Annoyed with Dad as I toweled off, I'd finally come to the real core of my emotion: it was chagrin. A characteristic of my father's poetic yearning that I deplored was his inflation of what was not truly worthy of poetical glory as though it were. Part of Dad believed he had the capacity to *make* things poetical that weren't—an occupational hazard of the rhapsodizer.

Yet I had done just exactly the same thing. I had been more concerned to make our meander in the fog a scene from some Horatio Hornblower novel than to decently and frankly communicate with my father. And more to this: I had tried to blame him for the consequences.

Today my most enduring, baseline image of my father is of him standing at *Reve's* helm, gazing forward through her open port light, guiding her to the next bell buoy. He is not looking at me. I am staring at him, endlessly, with fascination, compelled to absorb his every act and, if possible, his every thought.

Some of the things I see I dislike, yet at the same time I adore them, for they are just Dad. I dislike his shabbiness of dress; the poetical happenstance and joie de vivre of his inexact navigation; his incompetence with machinery; the way he drones on about the "dangers of the sea" to try to convince us that it would be prudent to cut short the cruise—when in fact he is just bored; the conditions are perfectly safe, the *actual* danger from his wobbling pipe as he leans casually over the open fuel tanks when gassing up at the Bucks Harbor fuel dock.

One of Dad's qualities that I absorbed was his attitude toward money. Of course, money is a practical thing, but Dad was not a practical man. For him—and he educated me on this, too— money was emotional. Remember how the apple does not fall far from the tree?

Once at Undercliff, Mom and Cal Lowell and I were sitting out front in the Adirondack chairs while Dad was down on the beach securing our launch to its outhaul. We had been out on the bay watching the sailboat races. Cal had a grand way about him, sitting in the sunshine, for he gestured widely with his arms and tossed his head of unruly hair. I knew Cal well, and so I'd understood what was behind the occasional glances between Dad and Mom earlier that afternoon while Cal waxed increasingly loudly. They were concerned that he might be entering another manic phase. Cal suffered from bipolar disorder, and his friends were ever vigilant to monitor his ups and his downs.

Now ashore, we were watching Dad do his nautical tidying up on the beach through a scrim of Mom's roses. Dad finished with the launch and walked toward us across the stones, lugging the empty lunch basket. Carrying on the conversation, Mom opined, "There's too much worrying about money."

"Oh, Betty, there's nothing to worry about with money," Cal replied.

Mom smiled. "That's okay for you to say. You're a Lowell."

"Still true."

"But how do you do it?"

"We always have someone else to look after the stuff, that's all."

Dad arrived and put the basket down on the front stoop. He looked a question at Mom, to catch up with the conversation. Mom said, "We're discussing freedom from money worries for artists."

Dad smiled. "Money is the devil."

My fellow students at prep school and I had been required to read the Bible, so I interjected, "No, Dad. I don't think that's it. I think what the Bible says is that it's the *love* of money that is the root of evil, not money itself. That's where the evil comes from—from the love of it."

Dad included Mom and Cal in his smile. "We have an expert!"

I laughed. "Well, that's what I think it says anyway."

"But how do you get some?" Dad, who had married some, tossed me this challenge. "That's the eternal question."

"You could *make* a lot of it."

I sensed this came out as a challenge to Dad, so I tried to soften it by adding, "That is, if you want a lot of it." Then I pressed forward with my case. "Even poets can make a lot of it. Jim must be raking it in." I was referring to James Dickey, whose novel and movie *Deliverance* were hot right then.

"Oh, Jim!" Dad tossed his hand.

Mom pushed in too. "Or think of Ted. Just because he was one year ahead of you at Dartmouth doesn't mean he's any better than you. Think of how he's doing." She meant Theodor Geisel, aka Dr. Seuss. "You could do that, too, you know. Why don't you write something that *everyone* wants to read?"

"It's doggerel."

"Of course it is. But it sells."

"But Betty, you went to Smith. How can you say such a thing?"

"My brother would tell you: sell more of what sells."

"Don't let's talk about your brother!"

"But you know what I mean."

"Cal, help me here. Shall we write doggerel?"

"Of course not! Write as obscurely as possible. That's what we'll do. Make them come to us."

"Yes, Cal. That was one of my lessons long ago. You remembered! It's good when the student surpasses the teacher. It's true: the reader must come to the poet."

*   *   *

That conviction—that the other person must come to the poet—was exemplified to me during an event from our DC days.

The big news in Washington when we were there was that Kennedy had won! Kennedy was breathtaking to the artistic crowd—his youth, his energy, his vocal ability, his beautiful wife, his sophistication, his small children in the White House, his sympathy with the arts, his request that the nation's most prominent elder statesman poet deliver a poem at the inaugural.

Everyone my family knew among the artists was agog.

As Number 482 (as I recall it, possibly incorrectly) on the official government protocol list, my father was automatically invited to all official government events with at least that many guests. Consequently, Dad and Mom attended the Kennedy inaugural ball, our family had close seats at the inauguration ceremony itself, and afterward we were transported quickly from the inauguration so that we sat across from the White House in the official reviewing stand during the subsequent parade.

It snowed in Washington the day before the inaugural. Nothing by New Hampshire standards—only about five inches—but enough absolutely to paralyze the poor city that was about to throw a big party. It took me six hours to get home from school that day on the bus, a trip that usually occupied about forty minutes.

Scores of artistic types were in the city, parading in and out of our house in Georgetown. My parents, as always, were loving it. Many artists had been invited to the various balls, but the snow had threatened their finery. I remember my mother hovering very much around baseball maven Marianne Moore, whose 1951 *Collected Poems* had won a hat trick—the Pulitzer Prize, the National Book Award, and the Bollingen Prize, all for the same book—but who was distraught at the inadequacy of her little gold pumps.

But the *real* news was that Frost had spent several hours that afternoon with Kennedy himself! Closeted together. Just the two of them.

It was ecstasy to realize that very shortly Frost would arrive at our house, and we would be able to quiz him about the new celebrity. What might Kennedy have said? How had Kennedy looked? Had Robert met Jackie? What—oh, what—was Kennedy *really* like?

In due course, Robert did arrive. We had a red armchair in the living room, and Robert settled himself there.

Imagine, just an hour before this he had actually been sitting in private audience with Kennedy! Why, you could practically feel the aura still quivering around him!

We were in a circle around the old poet, eyes wide, avid, lustful of news.

"What did he say? Oh, please tell us, Robert, what did he say?"

Pause. Twinkle. Lift of the eyebrow, slight cock of the head. "Well . . ."

"Oh, please! Robert, don't tease! You must tell us: What did he say?"

Pause.

And then, Robert being Robert, in sonorous voice—"Of course, I did all of the talking."

Even the *new president* must come to the poet!

*　　*　　*

And, speaking of Frost, so must I.

In seventh grade, we studied "The Road Not Taken." It's the poem about two paths diverging in a yellow wood, where the speaker, the poet, must select which path he should take. The last couplet is what everyone remembers—

I took the one less traveled by,
And that has made all the difference.

My teacher told us that the couplet extols Frost's prescience in selecting his own way—the way less traveled—over the ordinary, the more heavily worn path. But I was struck with another idea.

Three times earlier in the poem, Frost makes it clear that the roads were not different in wear or attraction. Poets don't waste words. I knew this from Dad. So here is what I figured. If Frost tells us three times in so short a poem that the paths are similar in wear, but then, at the end, he refers to one of them as being the path less traveled by, he must want us to notice his reversal. He must mean something *poetical* about his reversal, and he must want us to focus on the reversal.

Here's how Frost tells us the paths are the same—

Then took the other, as just as fair

and

Though as for that, the passing there
Had worn them really about the same

and

And both that morning equally lay
In leaves no step had trodden black

I was delighted! Frost was being subtler than my teacher imagined. Frost was saying two things, not one, and the saying of both of them in so short and seemingly simple a poem made the final couplet more interesting than my teacher supposed.

As I sat in class and listened to my teacher, it came to me suddenly what Frost might actually mean by his rhetorical and poetic reversal. I was only fourteen years old, but I could imagine a time when, later as a man, I might reflect backwards upon a moment when I had made a life's pathway choice. Reflecting back, then, I would need to acknowledge that the choice I had made precluded my choosing the other pathway instead. Then

I might congratulate myself on the wisdom of my choice. That was as far as my teacher's interpretation of the poem went, for after all, Frost had become a prominent man by following his poetical choice.

But instead, here is what flashed into my mind: Frost is teasing our imaginations to discover something more profound. Here's Frost's setup. Each pathway is equally used. Once we choose, there is no going back to take the other. Once we choose, we make further choices ("way leads on to way"). Finally, the pathway we choose is the one *less* traveled by, and it is also the pathway that makes all the difference.

How to solve Frost's riddle?

Here's what I realized. The poem is not about Frost's poetical choice, as my teacher supposed. The poem is about *everyone's* choice. *Everyone's* chosen pathway is the road less traveled by. Every one of us inevitably takes the road less traveled by *because no one else except ourselves could have chosen that particular road*. And therefore *each* of our pathways, individually chosen by each of us, upon which we now muse philosophically, makes all the difference.

The poem is about *us*, not about him!

I was almost breathless with excitement about my idea. Our homework that evening was to prepare ourselves for discussion of the poem on the next day. So when I went home, I asked Mr. Frost—who had stopped by for dinner—what he thought of my idea. I had always liked Frost, who had that granite face and unruly shock of white hair. Particularly I liked him because he played his part as the gruff New England versifier very well, but with a Yankier and Yankier twinkle in his eye.

And there were times when his eye would catch mine, and

he would shoot me a dart that delighted me because his dart told me how much fun he thought all of this was.

Gratifyingly, in his Robert-like way, he responded to my interpretation by saying, "Good, Dikkon." Then he smiled. "You've said it almost as well as I did."

Thus armed, I went to school with every expectation of heroism. English class came; we took out our books; my teacher asked if anyone had ideas; I raised my hand; I was called upon.

"Well, as a matter of fact I was having dinner with Robert Frost last night, and he said . . ."

It was a disaster.

My teacher could not have been less interested to hear something that came from so dubious a source as the author. I was soundly snubbed. I was made to sit down and was not called upon through the rest of the day.

Ah! How fickle is fame . . .

CHAPTER ELEVEN

When I was young teenager, I lied. Among the others of my sins at that time, lying was the most comfortable for me. It challenged my vanity the least.

I lied about 10 percent of things and was outraged when my father and my mother mistrusted me about the 90 percent that remained. Lying had dogged me hard for perhaps three or four years, until one particular time when, at fourteen, I lied one final time to Dad.

My best pal, Steve, had given me a cherry bomb. This was very cool. Our brownstone in Georgetown had a deck off my bedroom, which was on the second floor at the back. From the deck, I could look down onto our garden.

When Steve gave me the cherry bomb, I had an inspiration. That night, I would light the bomb in my bedroom, stroll onto the deck, and toss the thing into the garden, just to see what would happen. It was a great plan, and I was excited. The trouble with my plan was that I didn't know anything about fuses.

Late that night, while sitting on my bed, I lit the fuse. It burned extremely fast. Before I could even think—to say nothing of taking my leisurely stroll—the fuse was almost gone. Panicked, I jumped up and threw the cherry bomb toward the open deck door.

BANG!

Seconds later, my bedroom door slammed open. My enraged father, in pajamas, charged into the room. The room reeked of gunpowder.

"What was that? Did you do that?"

"No."

Wham!

My father hit me across the face with the back of his hand so hard that I staggered and fell back onto the bed.

"Don't you EVER lie to me again!" Slam of the door. He was gone.

I never did.

I cannot remember a single instant when I loved Dad more deeply or more profoundly than I did at that moment.

The thing was . . . Dad never hit; he was a poet. Mom? Now and then, when Gretchen or I needed it: on the tush, with the back of a hair brush; but Dad—never.

Granted, Dad probably would not have hit me had I not wakened him from a deep sleep and scared him half to death. Normally, he would have sat down on my bed and psychoanalyzed me. But what I needed in that moment was the alpha father, and I got him. Like many other young males, I was a cocky kid who needed to be struck down, just as we humans, I am sure, must seem now and then to God to be cocky kids— so totally certain in our self-admiration, so dismissive of the consequence of our sin, needing now and then to be struck down.

Where had this cockiness come from in me? Earlier in my life it had not occurred to me to challenge my father. Yes, I might be naughty—but lie? To lie is to challenge. It was clear to my addled brain that lying was disrespect, yet I did it anyway. I got away with disrespect, until the cherry bomb.

Looking back on it now, I perceive that Dad honored me just then. I know he loved my testosterone-flushed psyche for what glories and agonies it foreshadowed for me, about which he knew and I did not yet.

His son was becoming a man!

*　　*　　*

As the son in a literary family, I met Oedipus early. Before puberty, I didn't understand the sleeping with my mother part, but the murdering of my father part—*huh!* That was appalling enough, and yet authentic enough, to make me shiver. Not *Dad*, of course; certainly not! But there was about that Oedipus story an awe—this was mythmaking with a punch!—and it caused my insides to roil.

Hearing of it talked about, I encountered something primitive inside of me, something whose fetid breath made me gag. Some stupefying Beast lurked just behind the jolly facade of my Eberhart antics. That Beast tightened my throat, and it tightened another part of me of which I had recently become more aware, a part whose hot tightness I liked.

Panting through my mouth, sometimes with a little drool, I would go out quickly into the woods by myself and shoot action figures off of rocks with my gun. It was only a BB gun at that time . . . but still. I hoped to hurt those figures. When I picked them up afterward, I enjoyed seeing the dents.

I knew this pressure in my gut was what happened to Dad sometimes, and that his way to relieve its explosiveness was not to shoot but to create. It was elemental between us, this visceral knowledge I had of Dad's need, and of his will, to create. When pressure was intense in him, something new must be made to happen. Random words must become "The Groundhog." Tension in the house between Dad and Mom must become, by his charm, soothing laughter instead.

But as a youngster I knew, also, that the need to create could go wrong. A bad poem might come instead, whose music—as it were—was discordant clang.

If God, while intending Adam, should have created Satan instead, it would not have been a righteous creation; it would have been a clang. My father created me, molded me, and taught me, and once—when I needed it—he slapped me down. As he forced me forward, sometimes he slipped in his effort, and instead of making music, his effort went awry, and there was a clang.

I hated those clangs, but the effort of the men behind me— that is, of my father, and of his father, and of his father, all the way back to Eberhart the Noble sitting on his throne in Stuttgart in the scarcely imaginable thirteenth century—that effort, too, tensed me up.

And more to this: Eberhart the Noble had a father, who had a father, who had a father, who eventually was our very first father—our very first father, Adam himself, who was pushed into existence—fearfully and wonderfully made—by the very breath of God.

Dad let his pressure out by creating with his words, but I fell flat when I burst; I made nothing new: dead action figures, yes, but so what? Hair was growing on my chest. I could make a big bang by punching a door, but I had no words of my own. When later I became an actor, the words I said were just words from Shakespeare, Chekhov, Bolt, Ibsen, Albee, Miller, and Brecht.

Dad—that robber—had already used up all the words.

In the meantime, on the night of the cherry bomb, when I needed it much, Dad showed me the Lion Father and the backside of its paw.

*   *   *

A particular way Dad honored my testosterone-flushed psyche was to protect the icons of my young maleness against my mother's occasional attempts to clear them away. Living in Washington and being deemed old enough to make my way, alone, around the city by bus, I often went to public buildings after school. The FBI was a special target. I took the FBI tour so many times that some of the agents began to know me. The best part of the tour was what happened at its end. For then we descended into the basement to the firing range. There the agents fired their weapons for us at paper targets with life-size human silhouettes. The best of this good time was the last demonstration—the tommy guns. I loved those tommy guns then—and still do today.

There's nothing like a tommy gun to shred a target, especially if you have learned how to restrict its muzzle from moving up and to the right.

Since I was known by some of the tour guides, now and then they would retrieve the targets, riddled with bullet holes, and present them to me as souvenirs. I posted these grisly trophies on my bedroom wall. In my aesthetic view, they perfectly complemented my single most important objet d'art.

At the head of my bed I had enshrined a large poster of Sophia Loren. She was wet and angry, but she was the absolute perfection of womanhood nonetheless. Now and then, Mom would bemoan my man-cave decorations, but although she got her decorative way in most of the house, Dad held firm on his determination that I should command my own private walls.

Despite my gratitude to Dad for his support, I was plain angry at him too. Case in point: it was a rule of our house that I must wear a sport coat for nightly dinner at our dining table. As a young teenager, my fury at the injustice of this stupid rule seethed within me. Can you believe it, not one single one of my pals was tyrannized in this way!

One night I arrived with no jacket, and a fierce row occurred between Dad and me. In the end, I was banished to my room. Now, I was a strapping guy, and my anger was so powerful that I smacked my fist through the door of my bedroom, cracking its solidity with a single blow.

Silence from downstairs.

What must I do to make him grapple with my rage—kill somebody?

"I am at war with you!" I shouted. "At war!"

What Dad did about my shattering fury was to be Dad. "Ah, youth," he glowed the next day and patted me on the back. "What energy! What purity of emotion! What muscles! Hurrah!"

This made it worse.

If he wanted to defuse his emotions by poetizing them, then fine. But he had no right to defuse mine.

Mine belonged to me!

A few months later, Dad taught me something about the difference between anger and hate. As a poet, his teachings were oblique. As his son who loved him and who sought to catch up with his meaning, even in poetry, I listened hard. Sometimes his oblique teachings worked. And once, I got the back of his hand—which also worked.

Dad and I were sitting on *Reve's* afterdeck at anchor off Pond Island, several miles seaward from Undercliff. Everyone else was ashore—the women, the dogs, the children—enjoying the picnic. I was a man, so I had stayed aboard while Dad smoked a pipe, and I had coiled down all the lines in the hope he might notice.

Dad wore his long-billed fisherman's cap, a discouraged sweater, ratty khakis rolled to his knees, and sneakers with no socks. His World War II German binoculars hung around his neck. Lieutenant Commander (retired) Richard Eberhart, United States Poet Laureate, serving at the pleasure of President Eisenhower, himself a former military man, gazed over the placidness of East Penobscot Bay, and growled.

"It took us a long time to learn how to hate."

He was speaking about the war, a rare event. I was profoundly still, not to break the spell. I was hungry, you see; I was famished for truth.

"We are not of the hating kind. We were angry, oh, yes. That was easy. It was easy to be angry. But the Germans," he said, "they were better than we were, better soldiers. We respected the Germans—after all, Goethe, Beethoven. The Japanese were just a horde. We hated them first. It took us longer to hate the Germans, but we did it, finally." He looked elsewhere. "You don't go to war out of anger."

There was a long silence.

Then he looked back at me.

"You go to war out of hate."

He knocked the ash of his pipe overboard against the gunwale. "And we are not of the hating kind," he repeated, still looking at me. "We are not of the hating kind."

By that time in my life, I knew my father's war poems more deeply than by heart—by soul perhaps. I was beginning to understand their passionate plea that God explain and not hide his ineffableness behind an indifferent and especially not behind an ironical cloud. I was beginning to understand their anguish at the snuffing out of the lives of the young machine gunners my father tutored. I was beginning to understand their horror at the seductive beauty of tracer rounds—designed otherwise to kill—as they arched elegantly and silently at a distance and under a slender moon.

Calm now, when it was just Dad and me, and on the sea where I was masterful and at home, Dad was for me at that moment an adored and a supreme amalgam. He was a poet of Blakean fire; an aggressive and razor-edged intellect; a ruminator who burrowed down into the muck and found there a jewel and tossed it—with fanciful élan—into heaven.

And he was also a naval man who knew despair over a list of names whose faces he could not recall, but they had gone to early deaths, who defended their nation with machine guns on navy bombers, and whose marksmanship was my father's responsibility.

My father stood. "Enough about hate. Let's join the ladies ashore."

"But what happened then?"

Dad looked a question. "Then?"

"Then. When we learned to hate. What happened then?"

"Then we won."

CHAPTER TWELVE

A funny moment of international literary contrast occurred one time when the famed Russian poet Yevgeny Yevtushenko was visiting the United States and came to our Washington house for drinks and dinner. This was during the period of the so-called "Khrushchev thaw," after the Soviet premier had denounced Stalin, visited Beijing, and then come to visit President Eisenhower in our country.

Yevtushenko managed to tread a fine line between denunciation of past Soviet crimes against humanity and acceptable approbation of Communism. As a consequence, he was allowed to travel internationally more than many Russian writers, and Dad was his host in Washington.

Before Yevtushenko arrived at our house, I remember one of those exasperating arguments resulting from Mom's sense of humor and Dad's sense of decorum.

Mom wanted to invite James Angleton to the dinner as well. Like many of Mom and Dad's acquaintances, Angleton was a poet, which is how their friendship had begun. He would come

around from time to time for a drink and to talk poetry with
Dad and to joke with Mom, who shared his sense of humor.
What ignited this particular argument, however, was not the
fact that Angleton was a fellow poet but that he was chief of
counterintelligence for the CIA.

Just imagine the scene!

"Betty, I forbid it."

"But, Richie, it would be such fun!"

"No. Absolutely not. How could you even think of such a
thing?"

"I want to hear what Jim says about the party afterward.
Wouldn't you just love to know?"

"No, I would not love to know, and it's absurd to think
about it."

"Oh, pooh," and Mom stomped back to the kitchen.

Maybe Dad was right. Maybe it was better that Jim not
be present. Yevtushenko was accompanied everywhere he went
(and I mean everywhere, into each room) by a commissar whose
function it was to make certain that the exuberant poet didn't
defect or otherwise embarrass the dignity of the Union of Soviet
Socialist Republics.

The humorlessness of this Soviet functionary was ludicrous to
my mother, who I'm sure would have loved to nudge Jim about
it and to share a wink. The man was a lump in a shiny, plastic-
appearing suit, and he glowered in the corners of our living room
and dining room and smoked incessantly—not American ciga-
rettes, though they were far tastier than his Russian ones, as my
mother pointed out to him when she offered him a pack.

But Mom was always able to see the other side; that was
the key to her humor. Though the commissar was ludicrous,

at the same time, he touched Mom's heart. After the party was over, she expressed her sympathy for him. The poor man, she surmised, must have been witheringly, even agonizingly, ill at ease in our capitalist and degenerate household, where people just chatted and laughed and enjoyed life for its beneficence.

All during dinner, Mom tried to make the commissar bend. My mother was a fan of the Greta Garbo movie *Ninotchka*, and she thought that there must be a way to get the commissar interested (figuratively—for those of you who have seen the movie) in a new hat. But the man's spine was of cold steel. None of Mom's humorous blandishments made the slightest impact on the rigor of the Union of Soviet Socialist Republics.

The person who was most deeply affected by the dinner, however, was my father. I remember Dad and Yevtushenko making a production of signing and exchanging copies of their poetry books for one another. Dad, whose books were selling decently at that time, asked Yevtushenko how many copies of this particular book he had sold in Russia. His response: about three million.

Dad was stunned—*three million?*

For months afterward, Dad extolled his new friends, the Russians, for their poetic sensitivity. What a people they were, the Russians! Ah, the Russian soul! How magnificent that millions—*millions!*—of Russians read poetry as they mucked their fields and pulled their turnips! But then someone suggested to Dad that those millions of Russians might just have been told to buy the book, or else.

That deflated Dad, which made him particularly vulnerable to the next Russian crisis. Not long after the Yevtushenko dinner, a box showed up in the mail at Dad's Library of Congress office. It was a brown-paper parcel about the size of two loaves of bread. The wrapping was dirty and ripped. There was no return address other than something incomprehensible, written in Russian.

Dad checked. The box did not tick.

But Dad was alarmed. Perhaps something had been said at the Yevtushenko dinner that had offended the USSR. If so, the package might be a bomb. No, it did not tick, but things in the assassination business were probably more sophisticated by now.

What should Dad do? Maybe he should call someone at the FBI. Or Jim! "Maybe I should call Jim," Dad suggested. Jim would know what to do.

However, the next day, with calmer heads prevailing (particularly Mom's), Dad very gingerly snipped at the paper until it peeled away. Only when Dad saw what was inside the package did he remember that another of his new Russian friends, the novelist Mikhail Sholokhov, had promised to send Dad a boxed set of his novel *And Quiet Flows the Don*, for which, a few years later, he would win the Nobel Prize.

Afterward, it would sometimes hurt Dad's feelings when Mom would tell the story of the Russian package that was maybe a bomb.

"Why should anyone want to bomb Richie? He's just a poet."

"Just a poet? Just a poet? We poets used to be the principal advisers of kings!"

Mom could see that she had hurt Dad's feelings, so she stopped telling the story that way.

Of course, Mom was a wife. Many wives have a loving instinct to defend their husbands against possible disappointment by making certain their husbands are grounded in reality. (My wife, Channa, is another such wife.) In Dad's case, for example, when a new poem was turned down by some editor, and he was distraught, Mom would try to ground him by saying, "Richie, you think every word that drips from your pen is immortal. Well, it isn't." Sometimes this statement would relieve Dad's tension, but more often it would not.

These events occurred in the early 1960s. Ten or twelve years before then, when—headily—the war was over and all things seemed good with the world, several major poets poured out verse dramas. As Dad said, they were remembering ancient Greek drama and its impact on Athenian civil society five hundred years before Christ. Then, the dramas of Aeschylus, Sophocles, and Euripides truly shaped how the public thought.

Dad wrote verse drama too. He and two friends even founded the Poets' Theatre in Cambridge, Massachusetts, which still exists—more or less under its original mandate—to this day. Dad did not possess the playwriting excellence of T. S. Eliot or of Dad's friend Archibald MacLeish. But his motivation was the same: How shall we shape postwar society? One of the excitements of being United States Poet Laureate was that the title seemed to confer a shaping voice.

By the 1960s, however, the world had become more complicated than it had seemed after the war, before the Russians got the bomb. There was a new war, and while some readers continued to love poetry, poets did not play the tune to which the public danced.

Mom's statement was true. Not every word that dripped from Dad's pen was immortal—in fact, most words were not. But some words were, and it was those that kept him up late, striving to say what his muse gave him to say, for the betterment—as he thought it—of the world around him.

*   *   *

When we lived in Washington, I was at an age when being cool was important. Dad would chivy me with the statement that when he was young, the best thing for a teenager was to be *hot*. Dad was alarmed at the hands-off, pale-eyed, aloof adjective our generation had chosen to use when we approved of something. Dad thought our adjective betokened an unfortunate rejection of joy, and of élan, which would do our generation no good. Our laughter, he said, coming out of our linguistic base of *cool*, was too often cynical. Now, years later, I perceive that he was right.

Nevertheless, during those years when I lived in Washington, I was troubled by the worlds-colliding anxiety that my father himself might be . . . cool.

My *father*!

You see, Dad painted poetry with a broad brush. Not only did he draw *his* poets to the Library of Congress, but he drew mine, too. Occasionally I would come home from school and hear a tale from Dad about how he had spent that afternoon with a person whose face I knew well from a record album cover. How could this *be*?

Most folksingers passed quickly through Dad's office, or through our house, but some of them became friends. I came to know Mimi Fariña, younger sister of acclaimed folksinger Joan Baez, and her husband, Dick Fariña, whom I admired greatly. Dick used to read us sections of his almost-finished first novel, *Been Down So Long It Looks Like Up to Me*. Here was a handsome young fellow—not so *very* much older than I (yes, maybe ten years but not *fifty*!)—married to a seriously good-looking woman, who could sing (the two had recorded two excellent albums that bridged the start of folk rock), and he was finishing a novel I really liked the sound of.

Maybe *that's* who I could be!

But then I did not want to be Dick Fariña anymore.

I got a call from Mom. "I don't know if you know."

"Know what?"

"Dick Fariña just died."

"Died!"

"He was killed in a motorcycle crash. In California."

"But . . . but the book just came out."

"Yes. Two days ago. I'm sad to have to tell you. I know how much you liked him. He was doing a book signing and he rode away, and . . . well . . ."

I didn't know what to say. This was a death among *my* people. "Does Carolyn know?"

"I'm sure she does. She must."

"Oh, Mom . . ."

"Yes, my dear. I'm sad too."

Carolyn was Carolyn Hester, the folk music star with the mellifluous voice and the acoustic guitar, who had been Dick's first wife and with whom our family had developed a solid friendship in Washington. Carolyn, a Texan, had been a central figure in the Greenwich Village folk music scene in the early 1960s. She knew everyone, and she had even allowed the unknown Bob Dylan to play harmonica on several of the cuts on her third album. The closest I ever came to Dylan was Carolyn telling me funny tales of his borrowing her typewriter to knock out a song or two when he was penniless.

Later, when Carolyn would do concerts at Dartmouth and stay at our house, I would be her lighting engineer and man her spotlight from up on the light bridge. Whenever I manned Carolyn's spot, my friends noticed that she appeared to sing her most tender love songs right at me. I delighted in my friends' conclusion that she and I were . . . well, enough said.

For a time, when I was in college, I lived on the fringe of the folk music world, mostly doing lights, thanks to Dad's door opening for me back in Washington. The fact that I already knew some of these people made me able to talk easily with them, at least on the technical subject of their lighting. And I had one lively item that was purely my own to share with them and to laugh about. I had once dated Grace Wing. Who? You know, Grace Slick (née Wing) of Jefferson Airplane.

I remember once dropping her name to Art Garfunkel of Simon & Garfunkel. Our conversation went something like this—

Art, startled: "So you know Grace Slick?"

Me, complacent: "Yup. Dated her."

Art, curious: "How did that come about?"

Me, offhand: "My uncle and aunt live in Wilmette, Illinois, and I was visiting, and Gracie lived down the street, and she and I met, and she invited me to a party, and I went, and then we had a date—I don't remember, a movie or something. I liked her; she was funny and had a lot of friends."

Art, now to the important point: "Do you keep up with her?"

Me, punch line: "No, no. I just use her sometimes, with someone like you."

That made Art laugh. He and Paul Simon were the least affected by celebrity hauteur of the singers who streamed through. I could even talk to them directly about their lighting cues and not merely to their producer.

For a brief time, because I lit a number of their concerts, I was friendly with Ian Tyson and his wife Sylvia—a Canadian folk duo. They were easy to talk to also. They were outgoing and relaxed about any coming performance and seemed to truly enjoy their renown.

I'd love one more time to see the two of them do "Captain Woodstock's Courtship." The erotic tension between them, as Sylvia strutted around the stage singing of the seemingly impossible tasks that Ian, as Woodstock, would need to complete before she would lie one night with him on his old straw bed, simply crackled. Sylvia's required tasks led up to her final task, that Ian should "bring me a priest unmourned to join us one and all."

Sylvia's list of requirements worked for me. At the time, I so wished a woman to give *me* a hint too. I wanted to hear a woman as pretty and as strutting as Sylvia say, "Dikkon, bring me a priest unmourned to join us one and all."

If a woman were to say that to me, I just knew I would answer her with the same self-assurance as Ian did Sylvia.

CHAPTER THIRTEEN

If Dad brought me acquaintance with literary folk—however broadly defined—it was Grandmother who brought me the blandishment of the theater. Overall, Grandmother took special care that I should learn to be a gentleman. She loved the theater, and since, as a widow, she needed an escort to properly attend, she often chose me.

Etiquette and gentlemanliness were very important to Grandmother. For example, when she and I traveled together during my teen years to London, or Switzerland, or Spain, she honored me in a way that made me proud. She would slip money to me under the restaurant dining table, so that I, her escort, had the resources to pay for our meals. For Grandmother, I delighted to dress for dinner, which I hated to do at home. In Madrid and Cordoba, I used my prep school Spanish to order for her: "My grandmother will have . . ." I took care of our hotel bills and managed transportation and luggage. I reserved dinner seatings with train conductors, and I made Grandmother comfortable in the dining car while imagining we were aboard the Orient Express.

When I was very young, Grandmother took me to see *Peter Pan*, with Mary Martin (a girl, as I was offended to discover) playing Peter and Cyril Ritchard reveling in the best role in the show—Hook. I remember truly praying, just as hard as I could, for Tinkerbell to get well. I remember being enchanted with the flying. I was seeing it with my own eyes. It must be real.

I learned that anything—even an impossible thing—could happen behind the proscenium arch. What a wonderful world that must be. What a wonderful world into which to escape!

At first, Grandmother concentrated on musicals. She felt it was important that I be there when Carol Channing starred in *Hello, Dolly!*, when Rex Harrison was Henry Higgins in *My Fair Lady*, and when Robert Goulet appeared in that new show *Camelot*.

Goulet sang as grandly as everyone expected, but that other guy . . . my goodness, who was *that*? After the show, Grandmother took me to the stage door to see if I could get an autograph from—what was the name? Richard Burton. (I couldn't, by the way.)

But it was Mom who took me to *Oklahoma*, and did so twice—and she cried through most of it. "This is what we fought the war for," she told me, by which I understood her to mean we did it all for hope, and for goodness, and for loving-kindness, and so that Curly could still drive Laurey to the box lunch social dance in the surrey with the fringe on top.

Later, when I was in prep school and had begun to act myself, Grandmother's selections included edgier fare. For example, she took me to see *Equus*, which she had already seen. *Equus* has a nude scene, about which she gave me no warning. Grandmother and I usually sat in about the sixth row, orchestra center. I was poleaxed when the actress undressed, naked women at that time in my life being as rare as confidence. Grandmother leaned over and whispered, "Such troubled young people, but interesting, don't you think?"

I wasn't able to think.

Speaking of which, here's another time when I was scarcely able to think. One time in Switzerland, I ran into Brigitte Bardot—literally. Grandmother and I were swinging happily down a street in Gstaad, snow falling in puffy flakes, when I turned swiftly around the corner of a hotel and bumped into a woman wrapped in fur. We both sprang back; she was Brigitte Bardot.

I stammered; Bardot was amused.

Brigitte Bardot!

Grandmother, who took any moment to teach etiquette, whispered her desire to congratulate the sex kitten on a recent performance. But first, she said, I must make the introduction. After all, Brigitte and I had just become acquainted, while Brigitte and Grandmother had not. Try introducing your grandmother to the world's most famous wearer of the bikini, and doing so in French (which you scarcely speak), while still shivering at the feeling of Brigitte's fur (and what was bundled up inside of it) having been so splendidly slapped up against you.

This was one time when my *savoir* did not even have a chance to *faire*!

In other situations, Grandmother's etiquette meant that I did *not* converse with celebrities—she knew when to provide privacy. That same evening, she and I were ushered to a table at an elegant restaurant. She sat on the banquette; I was on the chair across from and facing her. I noticed that the waiter caught

Grandmother's eye and that she tilted her head ever so slightly toward me. This meant that I was to receive the host's menu and she the subordinate one. Only the host's menu showed the prices of the dishes; hers did not—for, after all, I was her escort.

I had just adjusted to this nicety when another couple was brought to sit at the table next to ours. A young and very beautiful woman was seated on the banquette next to my grandmother. Her escort sat in the chair facing her, just as I was facing Grandmother. Reluctantly, I drew my eye away from the beautiful woman and glanced at the man beside me. The elegant British movie star David Niven, one of my favorites, was sitting no more than four feet from me.

And there David Niven sat through the next hour and a half. He and his dinner companion carried on a lively conversation, as did Grandmother and I, and not by the slightest glance did Grandmother interrupt their privacy. The eyes of the two of them—Grandmother and Niven—met only once. At one point, two excited diners descended on Niven to ask for an autograph. Politely, Niven complied. As he turned his attention back to his young woman, his eye met Grandmother's eye. With the merest tilt of her head and the slightest twitch of one eyebrow, Grandmother seemed to say, "What can one do?"

With the merest tilt of his head and the slightest twitch of one eyebrow, David Niven agreed: "Yes, what indeed?"

And then we ordered dessert.

*   *   *

Back in the States, when Grandmother and her theater group of aged ladies from Cambridge drove up to New Hampshire to see me perform Shakespeare on the prep school stage, I was gratified. More so, when they looked at me differently after the curtain came down, it meant a lot to me.

There on the stage at Holderness School, as Petruchio in Shakespeare's *Taming of the Shrew,* my character's taming of the shrewish Katherine had gone over very well with the audience. One of Grandmother's theater friends and a Lakeview Avenue neighbor—possibly my favorite of them all—said this afterward: "Dikkon, I could not take my eyes off you. I think you have a gift." She paused for a moment. "Do you think you might want to be an actor?"

This was heady stuff for a lad whose father was, until now, always the eye magnet.

My grandmother's friends were the first to make me feel as I did later when Alec Guinness or Jimmy Cagney or some other established actor would take my acting ambition seriously and give me advice.

But was I really to be an actor? Was I really to make a living by seeming?

*   *   *

It's because Dylan Thomas used to read me bedtime stories that I was later introduced to Alec Guinness.

In 1964, when I was a college freshman, Sidney Michaels's play *Dylan* opened on Broadway. I'd spent the last three years acting—beginning with the role of Petruchio. By college time, theater was pretty much all I did. Before I had even matriculated, I had done a summer of repertory stock work, doing three plays with equity actors and becoming acquainted with Blythe Danner, who did an absolutely hilarious Rosalind in *As You Like It.*

Blythe was a very concentrated actress, not to be distracted. Sometimes a subtext runs parallel with the actual play. The subtext is the surreptitious effort by the actors (usually it's the actors and not the actresses) to insert some distraction into the performance, which the audience won't see, but which will so crack up the victim of the joke that she (it's usually an actress, and the prettier the better) will need to turn upstage. You only turn upstage when you need to compose yourself . . . and therefore admit that the joke worked.

But Blythe was of steel. Whatever we did, however hard we tried—and after many performances everyone, by now, was in the battle to get Blythe to turn upstage—nothing we did worked. She was one controlled actress. Until the last try.

One set of *As You Like It* is the enchanted Forest of Arden. Rosalind flees there when she is falsely accused of treason by her uncle. The forest is where she meets the man she will love, as well as other colorful characters. The way we built the forest was to suspend many "tree trunks" by ropes from the fly loft, so the audience saw a deep and wide forest of trunks through which Rosalind and Orlando, her lover, could flit and taunt and flirt with one another. The tree trunks were stage flats—the flat "walls" used in stage scenery—one flat per tree. Each flat was about a foot wide. Their front sides were painted as trees, but of course their back sides (facing upstage) were not.

At a dramatic moment in the action, there was one particular tree trunk behind which Rosalind hid. She went racing silently through the forest, saw this particular tree trunk, and leaped behind it, only to turn instantly and peer out from behind it. In turning, her face was no more than six inches from the back of the tree trunk flat.

One of our conspirators was inspired to paste a *Playboy* centerfold on the back of the tree trunk, just where Blythe would see it as she turned.

It worked!

Blythe turned upstage!

(Probably nowadays this would be sexual harassment, but it was funny at the time, and Blythe did have a sense of humor.)

But let's get back to Michaels's play *Dylan*.

The second act of the play is set in our house in Cambridge. One of the scenes occurs in my bedroom. Dylan is alone in my room, with me in my bed—you don't see me in the scene; there's just a bed, and I don't have lines—and, somewhat drunk, he philosophizes about life with me, while downstairs Dick and Betty are throwing a party for him. Now and then, poet John Malcolm Brinnin, who directed the 92nd Street Y in Manhattan and was the first man to inveigle Dylan to come to America, pops into my room and complains that people are wondering where Dylan has gone.

Well, it is safe for Dylan to be in my room. People can't get at him. (And Mom can't reject him.) And I am easy to talk to. Eventually, though, he leaves and goes down to the crowd. In real life, I probably trooped after him and sat on the stairs.

It's not every day you find yourself depicted on Broadway, so our entire family went to New York for the opening. Friends of my parents from the war, the Clayburghs, who knew New York theater society well, arranged the outing. They came to the show also, and with them came their daughter, Jill, whom I had known and liked for a long time, and who was two years older than I. I remember being quite impressed with Jill this time, with her New York sophistication that so outshone my own. It had come to me during the past several years that girls are, well, intensely interesting. Perhaps because of this evening, the connection between Jill and the theater always seemed to me to be inevitable, and I enjoyed it later when I would come across her on the stage or in the movies, just as much as I enjoyed it when she would drop by at Undercliff.

Dylan was a success that opening night and ended up running for about 270 performances. After the curtain, we all made our way to an elegant Manhattan apartment and joined a throng awaiting the play's star, Alec Guinness. That man duly arrived, and Dad took me over to introduce Guinness to the very child he had been talking to onstage just an hour before, now all grown up.

Guinness was amused by this encounter, and he had the graciousness to quiz me about my acting and my career plans. We spoke for perhaps forty-five minutes, with interruptions. I was deeply pleased by the man's attention.

Back when Dad was not much older than I was that night, he had roamed in Ireland. For a while, he had hung around and dined with William Butler Yeats and his circle. Like Dad conversing with Yeats, I tried my very best to say things that wouldn't seem trite to this great actor. And Guinness left me with advice, good for any young thespian—and for anyone else, for that matter.

"Well, Dikkon, if you truly want to be an actor, then I charge you with these two jobs. First, think seriously if there is any other way—any way at all—by which you can earn a decent living, and if there is, then do that instead. However, if you simply must act, and there's nothing else that will satisfy you, then find the very best acting school you can and acquire the very best classical education. Don't spend your time on the new styles. Master the classics."

Turns out, I followed Sir Alec's advice. I did find another way to make a living. But I still acted for my career: salesmen, after all, are actors.

Once when we were doing *A Man for All Seasons*, and I was the Common Man, I reached into a drawer at a climactic moment for the paper I wanted to shake in the face of Richard Rich, only to discover there was no paper there. The set dresser had neglected to put the paper in the drawer beforehand. Nevertheless, I pulled that paper out of that drawer, and I shook it in Rich's face, and my point was made. After the play was done, I tried to laugh with audience members about that missing paper—but every single one of them had seen that paper in my hand. I had "sold" that paper.

Actors are salesmen. Salesmen are actors.

It was much easier for me to be someone else than to be Dikkon, whoever Dikkon might be. For example, when I was a college sophomore, I loved to do Dr. Astrov in Chekhov's *Uncle Vanya*. I loved to do Dr. Astrov because I was required to woo—and sensuously to kiss—a faculty-wife actress whom I found particularly attractive. While I had managed to kiss a few girls my own age, this kissing business was still a new game for me. The onstage requirement that I should kiss this woman, and do so convincingly, gained me experience yet required of me neither confidence nor responsibility.

A sweet deal for me!

And sweet for the audience, too.

Art makes us see things that we don't normally see. Art makes us see things that ought to have been. Art makes us see things that are coming but not yet. Art can even make us see things that are not there.

And here's one more nugget of acting advice, one of my favorites from among others. This one is from James Cagney, with whom—and with his pal, Robert Montgomery—I spent a rambling and conversational day on an island off the coast of Maine, meandering the beach and kicking up stones.

Part of the fun of being with Cagney was that he spoke in Jimmy Cagney's voice, as though it were natural for him to do so and not a clever mimic—which, of course, it was.

I'd been telling Cagney a little of my acting ambition. Cagney had catapulted to stardom playing gangsters and other bad guys, and he said to me, "Dikkon, just remember this. If you really want to act, for any young actor just starting out, crime pays."

*   *   *

Dad was the one who made these encounters happen. How could I not adore that guy, my father, who could orchestrate such meetings?

And yet . . .

As I began to envision making a success of an acting career, Dad's success once again eclipsed my own.

In 1966, I was playing Fluellen in "Hank Cinq" (theater jargon for the title of Shakespeare's *Henry V*). Fluellen is a smallish role, but that was okay because the play was the big production for that season. We did it on the big stage upstairs, with full sets, newly created period costumes, intricately choreographed battle scenes—the works. And I liked Fluellen for his bluster.

We were doing a semi-dress rehearsal (*semi* meaning we wore any clothes or swords that would restrict our natural movements—and to which we needed to become accustomed—but not the costuming that was merely decorative). Our director's voice suddenly boomed over the loudspeaker. "Hey, Dikkon. We just got a call. Something's happened to your father. You've got to be home right now."

Home was a mile away across campus. I threw off my cap and my belt and sword, and I ran hard.

Don't let him die before I get there!

There were lots of cars out front. There were people milling around. They didn't seem to be sufficiently panicked. I burst in, out of breath and sweated up, still wearing my pantaloons and stockings, but fortunately for my run, with sneakers.

I saw Mom. "What's happened? What's going on? Where's Dad?"

"Your father just won the Pulitzer Prize."

"What? The what?"

"The Pulitzer Prize. Your father just won it."

"The Pulitzer . . . um . . . Prize?" Maybe the shock had given him a stroke. "Where is he?"

"In the living room. Go congratulate him."

"You mean he's okay?"

Suddenly, Mom understood the problem. "Oh, my dear boy. What did they tell you?"

"Just that I needed to be home right away because something had just happened to Dad. I ran."

She twinkled. "You poor thing. That isn't the message I intended. How silly. Now go see your father." She shooed me out of the kitchen and went back to gathering drinks and treats for the parade of merrymakers who were trooping through the house.

I was the blustering, arrogant, warrior Fluellen—just off the stage, out of breath, and half in costume—whose father, formerly dead, had just won the Pulitzer Prize. With a cheer, I bulled my way through the crowd in the living room, stood next to my radiant dad, clapped him on the back, and announced to the room, "Next year, the Nobel!" Everyone laughed, and that was how I was quoted in the local newspaper the next day.

Here's the very best comment, though, from that whole afternoon. Hearing the commotion at the Eberharts', Martha, the daughter of our next-door neighbors, ran home and burst upon her parents to announce, "Mr. Eberhart has just won the Poet's Surprise!"

PART THREE

That morning at Small Point Baptist Church I was confronted by the God-powered imperative that I must act—but
I didn't know how. For years, intellectual diffidence had
been my comfortable cloak. We intellectuals don't need to
act; our work is to think.

For years, I had thought upon God. But that morning I
was struck by the certainty that God is not satisfied merely
to be thought upon. God demands action. And I did not know
how to act, at least for Him.

I knew how to act in some venues.

I knew how to act in marriage—sometimes. Though
now and then not. Sometimes my way to act in marriage
was, after a major argument, to go out into the night
in despair and to lie facedown on the lawn and to press
my face into the cold earth and to grit my teeth with
anguish.

I knew how to act as a parent—sometimes. Though now
and then not. But I felt I was surer of my footing when I

marched before my daughters than when I marched before my sons, and I did not know how to act to equalize my footing among all of them.

I knew how to act as a son—sometimes. Though now and then not. My mother was deceased, and my father lived in his retirement community, much closer geographically to Gretchen's family than to mine. I did what I could do to visit and to engage with him. But other times, I would just send him another (unneeded) flashlight and allow Gretchen to carry more of the administrative burden because she was closer by.

Now here's something else you need to know about me. At that time, as a Jew, I believed Jesus was a wise man, a stimulating teacher, etc. . . . but that he wasn't, you know, a manly man. There was something too elusive, too ethereal. He wasn't like the rest of us men. The rest of us men—if you're a man, you'll know this, and if you're a woman, you will too—we men run on die-hard batteries of sex and competition. Whoever Jesus may have been to those who "got it" about him, he was fey to me.

And the Resurrection? I knew resurrection was big for these people, but really . . . while the idea was poetical and stirring, in reality, it was preposterous.

So why on earth did a committed Jew of middle age cross the road one Sunday in March in Maine? After all, he was successful in his sales career, happy in his marriage, and delighted with his four congenial children. He loved where he lived, and he even had a little time for writing—to

cultivate the gorgeous words and rhythms his poet father
had planted in his brain while he was growing up.

So why did he cross the road?

He crossed the road because he was trying to struggle
free from his father so that he might someday be able to say
something of his own.

CHAPTER FOURTEEN

"Oh, thank God, thank God, thank God!"

Mom threw her arms around me and burst into tears. Then she reached with one arm and scooped my girlfriend into her embrace too. "Oh, dear God!"

My girl and I were scarcely out of our car, just back from our happy day.

Mom and Dad and several stunned neighbors were standing beside our garage. "There's been the most terrible accident," Mom cried, and her embrace tightened. "Oh, it's been terrible."

My life changed.

At that moment, my life changed.

I didn't know what had happened, but I *knew*.

A knife stabbed into my gut, way down low, and it tore upward, ripping its way into my heart, and it sliced my heart in two.

I didn't know what had happened, but I *knew*.

I had killed someone.

What I did not know yet was that I had killed more than one someone and that one of the someones I had killed was a bright-eyed, blonde-curled, jolly-joking, last-sight-waving-good-bye eight-year-old girl.

What I did not know yet—but I *knew*—was that the face of that bright-eyed, blonde-curled, jolly-joking, last-sight-waving-good-bye eight-year-old girl was now seared into the inside of my skull, burned there like acid, inside my forehead, where I would see it, without even closing my eyes, every single day during the next thirty-eight years of my life.

My life changed. At that moment, my life changed.

I didn't know what had happened, but I *knew*.

Satan smiled.

"Gotcha," he said, and he chalked up another soul that he had broken.

*   *   *

My girlfriend was my first deep love. I was twenty-one; she was twenty. I was an actor; she was a dancer. We met at a party in a loft in Cambridge, which I had not wanted to attend. She had not wanted to attend the party either. Each of us was there at the behest of a friend. It was summer. I was living at Grandmother's house and driving a cab in Boston and trying to finish a story about a young man who was looking for a way to get to sea with the merchant marine because he could think of nothing else to do with his life—trying to finish it before college started again for me in the fall.

Our eyes met; our friends were forgotten; suddenly, this was the finest summer of my life—better even than *any* Undercliff summer with *Reve*.

One day, later in the summer, she and I took the weekend off and drove to Hanover so I could show her Dartmouth and introduce her to my parents. My parents liked her at once. Well chaperoned, we had a fine night at our house, and in the morning, since we had heard about a picturesque antique train ride that could be enjoyed on a bright Sunday, we drove off to give it a try.

The train ride was indeed picturesque, and the antique quality of it was fascinating. One of its anachronisms was that with this train line, when the individual train needed to switch to another line, the points—moveable sections of track—were lifted and moved by hand as they had been in the nineteenth century. So the train would stop, the conductor would alight, he would manipulate the points so that the track was now aligned in the new way that the train was to go, and then he would climb back on board, blow his whistle, and the train would move along. We excursionists would watch all this out the window of the passenger car and remark to one another about the quaintness of it.

Aboard our train that day was a bright-eyed, blonde-curled, jolly-joking eight-year-old girl. She happened to sit in the seat ahead of us with her parents, and she and we became friends as we giggled and winked across the back of her seat.

My girl and I were in love; this little gal was jolly; the sun was shining; all was right in this most perfect of all perfect worlds.

When our train reached its destination, we all debouched and explored the area. After a while, we desired to take a return train, and the next one was just about to depart. That train was already full of passengers, so we ought to have taken the following train. However, the conductor of the returning train saw that we were in love and that all was right in this most perfect of all perfect worlds, so he allowed us to board his train and to take our places on the rear platform of the passenger car, which was his station too.

Our train pulled away.

And there she was! There was that bright-eyed, blonde-curled, jolly-joking, last-sight-waving-good-bye eight-year-old girl. She had run over to the train tracks and was waving to us.

"Good-bye, good-bye," we cried to her. "Good-bye, good-bye."

Along our way, as before, our train needed to switch to the other line. When the point-switching process was done, our conductor climbed back aboard our platform, blew his whistle, and our train started up. My girl and I were standing with our hands on the rear rail, looking back along the track where we had just been. The conductor was looking the same way too. Looking back along the track, suddenly I saw that the point-switching process had not been properly completed and that the rails were now misaligned.

I opened my mouth to call out, "Hey, that doesn't look right!"

But I closed my mouth. I was shy. I was shy to speak about anything except love in front of my newly loved girl. And any-way, the conductor—a professional of the line—was looking behind us in just the same way that I was looking, and he was saying nothing.

Ours was the most perfect of all perfect worlds. *Of course* the engineer of the following train would see the misalignment of the tracks, and he would stop his train in time.

I could have shouted, "Hey, that doesn't look right."

I could have.

But I did not.

The engineer of the following train did not see the mis-alignment of the tracks in time, and he did not stop his train in time. His train—the train on which my girl and I should have been barreling along—derailed and plowed into the earth and six people died, among them a bright-eyed, blonde-curled, jolly-joking, last-sight-waving-good-bye eight-year-old girl.

*   *   *

My girl and I took our sweet time getting back to Hanover. There was quite a lot of countryside to see, and I knew of a beautiful, secluded pond where I could stop, and where she would be pleased to admire the view. I did stop at the pond, and she did admire the view, and she let me kiss her—quite a few times—until both of us realized we had better stop that business right away quick. So then we moseyed on, meandering through small towns, perhaps—I don't remember—stopping for an ice cream cone.

Meanwhile, back home, the news of the terrible accident had broken over the radio. Jean, our next-door neighbor, rushed to our house. "Turn on the radio, quick!"

Aghast, Mom and Jean heard the news flash repeated. Another neighbor showed up at our door. "Didn't Dikkon and his girlfriend just take that train?"

"Oh, my God," moaned Mom. "Richie! Richie, come here!"

Dad held Mom. The neighbors stood around, supporting them. There was nothing to do—cell phones hadn't been invented. Hours went by.

"Oh, I can't stand it!" Mom cried.

And then, bold as brass, happy as clams, we drove up—and my life changed.

I wished that knife in my gut had *actually* bled my heart out.

CHAPTER FIFTEEN

Meanwhile, while wishing I were dead, I needed to do something to support myself during this dead life I was sentenced to lead.

Was I really to be an actor?

Acting offered me control.

I could control everything around me when I was in the theater. Once the rehearsals and the mistakes and the changes in direction and the responses to the stage notes were done, then there was just me—up there in the lights—saying things I knew how to say and causing the other actors to react as they had been instructed to react.

The only unknown was the reaction of the audience, and since I was good at what I was doing and took my job seriously and studied our art intently and deeply desired to give the audience a touch of this script's grandeur, or pathos, or irony, or whatever it was, the audience's reaction was almost always ideal.

On stage was the safest place I knew. Many other places were not safe like that. Places where classes met were sometimes not safe. Places where girls mingled were usually not safe. Places where men drank themselves into stupors were always not safe. Places—like my parents' dining table—where yet another of those poets was holding forth in order to impress my dad— those places were not safe either.

I was safe on stage, but was I to be an actor? One of my acting pals in college, Jerry Zaks—since then the winner of four Tony Awards—certainly was to be an actor, and a director as well. You could taste it on him, like salt. But was I to be one?

Anyone who has been an actor and has taken it seriously knows its seductive power. Standing there in the light, you are saying words you have perfected the saying of. You can't see each audience member, but what you can do is make all three hundred of them hold their breaths at the very same moment. And then you can make them cry.

You are at center stage delivering the last line of the play. You can feel tension in the audience. They ache with tension. Slowly, you speak the last line of the play except for its single, final word. Then you pause, and then you sweep your eyes across each of their eyes, as they sit there in the darkness, tight and waiting, and then—with a softened voice—you utter that single, final word.

The lights snap out. The play is done. There is an instant of silence. Then the applause swells, and it swells, and it keeps on swelling. And then the lights come back on, and you are lifted so very high that you are above (this is how it feels anyway), even for one moment, above even sin.

You are above the sin of killing an eight-year-old girl.

Addicting, that.

Addicting, that seduction not to be you.

Addicting, that seduction for Dikkon not to be messed-up Dikkon. Addicting, to be another Dikkon who is not messed up. Addicting, to be able to *prove* that Dikkon is not that messed-up Dikkon. This Dikkon is another Dikkon who has just made three hundred people cry by saying one single word.

It scared me, that addiction to seduction.

It scared me that I might become addicted to not being me.

It scared me that I might become addicted to trying to control everything around me. It scared me that I might become addicted to the attempted control of the uncontrollable.

Train wrecks are uncontrollable.

Then—then, when it mattered—messed-up Dikkon had not said that one single word.

Then—then, when it mattered—I could have said that one single word.

"Stop!"

That is that one single word that I could have said.

But back there on that train platform, I was playing to the wrong audience. I was playing to my girl and not playing to the whole wide world, which is filled with pretty little gals and with much else besides, all of which needs loving attention from me, all of which needs me to say one single word of truth—when it matters.

I would simply have to bear my sin after all. My artistic subterfuge of making three hundred people cry on cue was not enough to get me out from under the boulder of my sin. Better, I thought, to turn my back on this addiction to being someone else than myself and to figure out how to live within the world as it had actually been given to me by God.

But I was still an actor. I was an actor wherever I went. I couldn't help myself.

* * *

Let's call it—say—the summer of 1967, and I'm in Paris by myself. I am very conscious of being on the *terrasse* of the Dôme Café. I'm in love with the fact that I'm sitting on the terrasse of the Dôme Café. So much happened here, really, not so very many years before.

Right over there at that table—this is how I set my scene—right over there at that table, Modigliani, the great Italian painter and sculptor, sits with his lover, the French artist, Jeanne Hébuterne. This is just before he dies and she throws herself, nine months pregnant, from her father's fifth-floor bedroom window. Perhaps those two are not so famous in death as Romeo and Juliet, but still Modi and his lover are free—those lucky ones.

At that other table on that other side, I see Henri Cartier-Bresson, the father of photojournalism—an acquaintance of Dad's during our DC years—dallying with Caresse Crosby, while her husband, the poet and bon vivant Harry Crosby, looks indulgently upon their explosive love affair from the next table, glass in hand. Perhaps their affair is not as culturally famous as the affair of Héloïse and Abelard, the ideal among twelfth-century lovers, but Harry is soon to be free of this vale of tears himself. Dead by suicide pact—Harry and one of his many lovers, while his wife Caresse waits for him that evening at the theater. Harry Crosby's suicide was the champion literary suicide until Dad's friend Hart Crane, poet, jumped off the stern of a steamship in the Gulf of Mexico two and a half years later.

Crane's was the archetypal suicide for Dad. It was clear that artists, and poets, and bohemians, and absurdists, and other knights of Mankind Only—since there is no God—had this to say: "Why in the world not? Well, I mean it. My life is mine only, and I may take it away."

Their atheist conclusion, and their actions, horrified Dad.

I am on the terrasse of the Dôme, and I am not free. By negligent omission, as a killer, I have lost my right to be alive. Yet I do still find pleasure in life. I find pleasure being in Paris; it is my first visit. I am heavily mustachioed, like Hemingway—another champion literary suicide. When you look around, suicides seem suddenly to be everywhere.

I have no intention of suicide, but I am deeply wounded by my messed-up-ness, and my literary romanticism inclines me to muse upon the self-indulgent suicides of the life despisers, and the humanity despisers, and the God despisers.

My French is almost nonexistent. Still, I have a little playlet for myself to act out. I've just spent a week kicking around in the Spanish-speaking areas of Morocco. I am thrilled to be told by a Dôme waiter that he assumes I must, indeed, be Spanish, for I speak my hesitant French with that sort of accent.

Hot stuff!

At the table next to mine sits an American couple of Midwestern middle age, enjoying their European vacation. I have overheard them trying to make themselves plain when ordering, but I have, of course, disdained to assist them in any way. Certainly they are no fellow countrymen of mine!

After a time, I realize that the wife of the couple is trying to catch my eye. I deign to give her a slight nod. She rises and makes her way to my table. She does her best to communicate that she desires to sit at my table and to have her photograph taken with me by her husband. After all—this is the Dôme, and I am evidently an artist of some kind, and here we are in Paris.

Once I manage to grasp her meaning—her French is poor and, after all, I have no English—I gravely allow that this might be permissible.

The thing arranges itself. She sits; her husband manipulates the camera. *Voilà!* It is done.

Her thanks are profuse, and in them her husband joins. I am gracious, though cool.

"Harry," she says, nudging her husband, "he wants some money. Give him some money."

Harry has the obligingness to reach into his pocket and to withdraw a five-franc coin. He offers it to me, and with condescension that becomes me very well, I accept it.

I have a career!

I order another *vin*, and the sun smiles down on the intersection of boulevard Raspail and boulevard du Montparnasse. Later in the day, I will order an *omelette jambon avec pomme frites* (which is all I ate during my ten days in Paris because it was all I knew how to say), and the evening will come on with a smatter of new faces, like petals on a wet, black bough. (Poet Ezra Pound's phrase, not mine; but apropos.)

I believe Toulouse-Lautrec, in his disinterest, would have enjoyed me with a sharp pencil. (Another steal, slightly altered, from Dad this time.)

As a college boy, I am in Paris looking for something to say of my own. I want to stop reading lines. I want to stop stealing phrases. I want to say something that hasn't been said before.

Back in the States, though, I live onstage. At least, at single-sex Dartmouth, it is a way to meet girls without going through the horrid dating "scene." As it turns out, it isn't hard to meet girls in Paris, either—indeed, many girls come up and desire to meet me, for a fee.

But in Paris it is hard to find words to say of my own. I have no pal to go around with, and that may account for it. I have Paris, and I have my career, but I am mute.

Years and years before, Dad, pedaling south out of Paris on his way to Provence, had felt "a very god," as he put it. He wasn't very much older than I was, but he was already a songster entire.

*   *   *

What will Dikkon do? In my family, the question was a big one.

Back in the States, Dad sat me down. I suspect Mom had goaded him—"You're his *father*, Richie. He's lost. He doesn't know what to do. He needs to talk to you, not to me."

So Dad sat me down. He told me that his brother, my Uncle Dry, had chosen stocks and bonds. I knew this. Then he told me that Mom's brother, my Uncle Charlie, had chosen to stay in the family company and now ran it very well and had become very rich. I knew this, too. Finally, he told me that there were lots of businesses in which I could make my career. He said there was insurance. He knew men who had made a life in insurance. He said there was medicine—though he didn't think of me as a medicine type. He said there was law. He said I might be a law type; he would need to think about that. Then he got around to teaching. I was a natural there, he said. Teaching might be the perfect thing. You get three months off in the summer so you can do your other work too, if you are an artist of some sort. I could do some acting and still teach. I should think about that. Then he said we should go out to dinner, so we did.

(Stage-managing note: this conversation, Dad's and my single one of its type, took place in his and Mom's suite at Manhattan's Chelsea Hotel—they told me it was the same suite William Faulkner used to occupy when he was in town—when Dad was helping his bestselling-novelist friend Erica Jong finish a teaching stint at Columbia. Jong's book *Fear of Flying* was a delicious national scandal. I would have liked to meet her, but I was too shy to ask for an introduction from my dad because her book was famous for its . . . sex.)

What Dad did not know, and what I did not know how to tell him while we sat in Faulkner's suite, was that I wanted to be him. Well, not him *exactly*. But he, too, received that applause I knew the seduction of. And yet he was a regular guy—not as messed-up as me, of course, but messed-up enough.

Acting aside, for me, my real career choice was just fiction over poetry; that was all.

Recently I had reread all of Hemingway's short stories (for about the tenth time), and "Big Two-Hearted River" had convinced me of my goal. If I could turn away from theater, and if I could do the same thing Hemingway had done—metaphorically show my readers the sunlight dancing on the surface of the river while they were allowed to sense the power of the big fish down below—then, when I came to die, I should not have been hanging around and just breathing up the air.

I want to be you, I shouted silently to Dad, *but I don't need any more poets! Who I need is Hemingway*. Unhappily, that man's suicide had occurred five years before.

Still, Dad must have understood. He was awkward in his role

of The Father of Dikkon, but he was a kindly man when just being my dad. So, shortly after our talk about careers, Dad drove me over to introduce me to the former Hadley Richardson, Hemingway's Paris wife.

Hemingway's Paris wife was just then living on a hillside in New Hampshire. She turned out to be a nice-looking, middle-aged woman of pleasant mannerisms. I do not recall that she spoke much about her former husband during our visit. Perhaps she was content to leave the subject well enough alone, now that she was no longer tossed about in the wake of her preposterous, genius husband. Mostly she chatted about how her life had gone since Hem. I liked her.

As it happened, I had read a great deal about her former husband. Though fascinated, I did not like what I learned. I hated Hemingway's statement that a moral act is one you feel good about afterward. I hated Hemingway's need for a new wife at every shift of his literary career. Unlike some fawning critics, I felt the man's stylistic genius really was for short story only, though he translated it successfully into parts of his first two novels and into his Paris memoir. I deplored Hemingway's later life of parodying himself literarily, despite my sympathy with him for what I suspected was his terror that he had lost his muse, and that he had no power left—but that he still had his fame to feed anyway.

Intuitively, I knew about the anxiety of the artist whose youthful flair is subsiding into sometimes-forced reiterations.

At the time I met Hemingway's Paris wife, Dad was in his middle sixties. Dad had been respected in his field for more than thirty years. He had not yet won the National Book Award (though he would soon), but he had won the Pulitzer Prize

and the Bollingen Prize and the Harriet Monroe Poetry Award
and so on. Dad could open almost any literary or artistic door
he wanted to open, and he could—and did—bring Mom,
Gretchen, and me through that door with him.

Many other men in their middle sixties begin to think about
golf, or fishing, or moving to the sun, or volunteering at the soup
kitchen as ways to relax now that their work has been done. Dad
was not relaxing. He was still turning the stuff out as quickly as
it came to him—or as quickly as he could force it to come to
him. Off each new poem would go, with eager enthusiasm, to
this editor or to that one.

Dad lacked literary political intuition. Frost had more discipline as well as more literary political sense than Dad did. Frost
once told me that poetic genius is like mathematical genius. It
flares in the young, but an old poet must parse it out slowly and
carefully; there may not be much of it left.

Frost would hold a poem sometimes for years before releas-
ing it; Dad released his poems before their ink was dry. Frost
starved the critics, so they were eager for their next Frostian
meal. Dad flooded the critics, so even when they liked the look
of their next Eberhartian dish, their minds were on Maalox.

Dad won the Pulitzer because James Loughlin of New Directions Publishing would not let Dad push him around. Loughlin published a *selected* collection of Dad's poems, and only
he—Jay—was allowed to do the selecting. Bingo! The Pulitzer.

Dad's most frequently anthologized poem during the first
two-thirds of his career was "The Groundhog." He wrote it in
1934, when he was thirty and had found the dead animal in a
field in Pennsylvania. It's a death poem: Dad's greatest theme.

Dad told me that he wrote three poems that same day, all

of them seeming to him to be of equal power. He said he did not change a single word in "The Groundhog"—"Or maybe I changed one, but that's all." "The Groundhog" made my father famous, but the other two poems were scarcely noticed by the world.

Why?

Now and then he would go back and lay the three pieces of paper next to one another and gaze at them. Maybe, he thought, he might see something in the penmanship that would suggest why one of these poems was God-sent and the others were not, but he could never find a difference in the handwriting nor in anything else that was material. It wasn't the handwriting, or the ink, or the paper, or the time of day, or the angle of the sun, or the rumble in his stomach because he had missed lunch. It was something else—on a different plane entirely.

One of those three poems ought to endure in English literature forever. Two will not. Why?

It's a God thing.

By the 1980s, academic and critical taste had changed since Dad wrote "The Groundhog." That dead rodent had launched Dad like a rocket into the literary stratosphere, a great trail of fire burning behind him. Burning—that's the point.

When Dad wrote the poem, five years after T. S. Eliot's "The Waste Land" appeared, some within the literary world loved it that Dad and others challenged the cool rationalism of what they called "modernism" in Eliot and his new poem.

But times and tastes had changed since the 1930s and 1940s and 1950s, and the critics are self-appointed as the door wardens of literary immortality. They grind away and they grind away, very fine. For many critics in the last quarter of the twentieth century, modernism may have become passé, but its virulently ironic child—postmodernism—had won out entirely over hot passion.

It is the taste of the critics that controls who gets into the big new anthologies, and by the late 1980s and the 1990s, often the critics, like policemen, would pull my father's poetical car to the side of the road and chastise him for driving while innocent.

In the 1990s, when I was being hurt for Dad over his lack of inclusion in some important new anthology, he was in his own nineties. The burden of the past for my father was ninety years heavy. The events and urgencies and tastes and astonishments and agonies in which he had participated during his years were being forgotten by the world, faster and faster. Yet they were the facts of Dad's life which, to borrow from Frost's poem, had made all the difference. In a general way, Dad was loath that the world's knowledge of these facts should be lost. Yet what was most urgent for my father was not the loss of the facts but that we new people—we new people who have our own urgencies to attend to—we new people should concentrate on what remains permanent and does not disappear, and what is ever renewing.

Dad saw cultural taste about poetry change just as cultural taste about much else changes. He did not see, nor did he ever believe, that the urgency among poets to write poetry was changing. Poets write the way they write because they were put on earth—as Dad would say it—to write the way they write.

In his last published interview, when Dad was ninety-five, he said, "The young poet should go on writing poetry and finding out what is his true nature and what is his destiny. What is his soul. Since God Almighty has to do with all of us, this young poet is put on earth by the immortal Truth. But it is his human job to discover his human truth. There must be some kind of mystery in which Shakespeare became Shakespeare, Milton became Milton, Keats became Keats. How incredible that these people appeared on the face of the earth! But they did. But *why* did they? And isn't it strange. And is there any answer to it? Who can know?"[1]

Interviewers frequently asked Dad the question, "If you could go back and meet Shakespeare, what would you ask him?" Dad's answer was always the same: "Do you know you are Shakespeare?" Somehow a man born in 1564 in Stratford-upon-Avon, the son of an alderman and glove maker, became an ink-scribbling, theater-minded entertainer . . . and became Shakespeare. Just so, Milton became Milton, Keats became Keats—and Dad became, well, Dad.

What was I to become? By what becoming would I become authentically me?

I had one consolation in my confusion. Unlike Modigliani, Hemingway, Crosby, or Crane, at least I was still alive and was free to craft an answer to my question.

CHAPTER SIXTEEN

"So this is the very boy!"

Marie Rexroth stood on the landing outside her house, high on a slope among eucalyptus trees, north of San Francisco Bay. She was a slender figure of middle age, swathed in offhand and colorful garments, attractively casual to my prim New England eye.

"Yes," my mother called up to Marie. "Yes, he is the very boy!"

Mom and Dad and I had just emerged from our car, which we had parked in the small opening among the trees perhaps one hundred feet below Marie's house.

Marie watched us for a moment more. She assessed me with a speculative eye. "Your son looks very like you, Dick." Then she smiled. "Come on up."

We climbed Marie's long, wooden staircase through woods that would never see snow. The house felt almost like a tree house. Marie gathered us in and hugged my parents. Then she turned to me. She put a hand on each of my shoulders and looked me in the eye. "How old are you now, young Dick?"

She spoke as though she knew me, when she did not. "Twenty-three."

"My goodness," she said.

She turned and stood beside me. She had one arm across my back. She clapped me once, firmly, on the shoulder. Then she stood away.

She looked at Mom and Dad. "All those many years ago," she said. And then she shook her head, and then she served lunch.

By dessert, we were relaxed and sprawling. Marie remembered: "When first I saw you, Dick, in your navy whites, when you and Betty knocked on our door. Weren't we aghast!"

Mom laughed. "We hadn't known how to dress. What does one wear to a beatnik party?"

"Not navy whites!"

"Handsome as they are," Mom reminded us, twinkling at Dad.

"Yes," Marie agreed. Then, speaking of her ex-husband, she went on. "And I could tell what Kenneth was thinking when you two were at the door. I could tell what he was thinking."

Dad was happy to take Marie's bait. "What was he thinking?"

"This—military man at the door," she grinned. "He was thinking that this military man can't be *Eberhart*." Marie touched Dad's arm. "You were supposed to be a cadaverous aesthete with burning eyes and the haunted air of a Baudelaire." She broke off. "Hey—good!"

We all laughed. Dad was having fun. "Ha-ha!" he said in his grand-gesture way. "Ha-ha."

"What Kenneth wrote about you, Dick—'obviously the finest poet of his generation'—that's what he said, Dick, and he meant it."

Then, Marie's face became more inward. She looked down at the table for a moment. Mom made her *mmmm* sound, her soothing sound.

Marie's ex-husband's poetry—Kenneth's poetry—often burned brightly to illumine the transcendental quality of married love. Fine; that was good in itself, as a theme for poetry. But there is the human side to poetry, which can complicate the pure art of the words. This woman who had just fed us lunch was the second of what, in the end, were to be Kenneth's four wives, each of them apparently his muse regarding the transcendental quality of married love.

I had much to learn yet about the beatnik way.

Then Marie took a breath and brightened and turned to me. "What about you, young Dick? Are you a poet too?"

"Um, I've written only one poem in my life."

Dad explained, "Dikkon is here to get a master's in theology at Berkeley." This was factually incorrect, but it was more-or-less true enough—for a poet. I did not correct him. It would have been pedantic to insist that it was a master's in psychology and religion at Pacific School of Religion (coupled with a master's of divinity), and not at Berkeley but just up "Holy Hill" from that university.

"Good for you," Marie asserted, "and to think that it all started in Inverness!" Then she looked at my mother and winked. "It was the lambs, Betty. That's what I said at the time. The lambs!"

Everyone laughed, though I did so awkwardly—I knew the reference from before, from my mother.

Mom belted a laugh. "The lambs! Richie, remember? It was the lambs!" Dad responded to Mom's effusion with a wave.

I felt torn. Of course, I desired to hear everything—every

item in the backstory. But I feared that, hearing the items, I might become even more tightly wound inside our family saga than I already was, and from which, at my age of twenty-three, I was doing my best to be unwound.

I had newly moved from New England to Berkeley—yes, for the degrees—but more so to make a life of my own, with my new and sparkling wife. My new and sparkling wife was not the woman of the train accident, though that woman had attended our wedding with a gracefulness that spoke well for her character. My new and sparkling wife and I were both of us too young, it is true, but we were full of beans just the same.

Shortly after we arrived in Berkeley and set ourselves up in a student apartment on LeConte Street, here came my parents, for ten days, to see our digs and to renew old friendships among Beat poets as well as among many other poets who were not Beats. As I have said before, Dad and Mom did not particularly care which school a poet was considered to be part of. Dad and Mom loved all energetic writers and refused to participate in literary war.

Before my marriage, Mom had her doubts about the union, and she shared them with me. Not Dad. The evening before my marriage, Dad sat me down. I expected his paternal advice, which I suspected, from Dad, would be positive. Dad liked my bride. She was pretty and funny and spoke French fluently and knew literature well and looked lusty and was endowed, not only with your basic female skeleton, but with all that other fancy stuff that comes along with it too.

Instead of advising me, which I desired, here's what Dad said: "You have more courage than I had when I was your age."

I did not feel courageous. I was excited, of course, for the morrow, but I was scared.

Dad went on. "I could not have done what you are about to do. I did have a candidate when I was a little older than you. We were in love," he smiled, "at least in an aesthetic way. But I feared that, if I had done what you are about to do, the poetry would stop."

Not advice, this.

I already knew about Louise. I already knew about Dad's and her two-year, epistolary love affair, across the Atlantic, between England—where Dad was at Cambridge University—and New Jersey—where she lived with her wealthy family. I already knew that Dad asked for "actual companionship," as he put it, but that she avoided it. Once, the two of them happened to be in Paris at the same time. Each knew that the other was there. And yet still—even in the City of Light—Louise avoided a meeting. Letters were better.

At Dad's insistence, finally, Louise did stage a meeting, this time on Sicily, at Taormina, on a particular esplanade beside the sea. She had thought it all out. She even went so far as to rename the two of them for their assignation. She would be Maia, and Dad must be Ricco. She would be standing watching the sun, wearing her special green dress, and he would approach her from behind, and she would sense his arrival, and she would half turn, and her hair would come free. . . .

Dad: "And the next ten days were heaven."

It amused me then to picture Dad back in London shortly after his tryst. He attended a show of the paintings of D. H. Lawrence. Dad spent an hour next to the man, saying nothing, too shy to introduce himself. So there was the burly Midwestern football player, just back from ten days of aesthetics on Sicily, lurking over the diminutive novelist, who, just at that moment,

I imagine—the timing is right—was probably dreaming up Connie Chatterley in his mind.

The literary world gives us such evocative snapshots, does it not?

I was susceptible to snapshots. I had inside me a whole scrapbook of snapshots. I treasured them with filial love. I loved Dad's stories of his Asiatic and European adventures, but I was burdened by them too.

How on earth was I to become someone other than a derivative edition of him?

*　　*　　*

The evening before our visit to Marie's, Dad wanted to introduce me to City Lights Bookstore. The store was thriving when we stopped by. It was lots of fun for Dad. I was happy to see Ferlinghetti, who owned the store and whom I had known and liked for several years. Then Dad and I ended our day at Fort Point in a soft San Franciscan fog.

Fort Point is underneath the massive south end of the Golden Gate Bridge. The Golden Gate itself is the narrow passageway through which all shipping must enter and exit the harbor. It is a spot filled with heavy tide flows, shrieking gulls, lolloping sea lions, and romance. It was romantic to me, anyway, because it was through this very passageway that Dad had shipped out forty-three years before, when he was almost exactly my own age of twenty-three.

Leaning against a post, Dad told me a little about the *West Faralon*, the cargo ship that he had boarded along the Embarcadero when he was an ordinary seaman with naught but a rucksack on his back, a copy of Shakespeare in his pocket, and the idea that he should end up eventually in England, at Cambridge. I had heard these tales before, of course, but standing as we were at the very spot where his adventure began, I was keen to hear them again.

By the time the *West Faralon* reached China, Dad could hand, reef, and steer (that is, work with the ropes, handle the sails, and steer)—he was an able seaman. The ship moved cargo from port to port, all up and down the China and Philippine Seas. My father learned how to stay out of the worst of port life—how to get a view of the mysterious East and not a knife in his ribs.

Moving heavy cargo is difficult, tedious, sometimes danger-ous work. In Dad's report, the crews who worked the cargoes and the derricks and the lines and did the chipping and the painting and the polishing of the brass were urgent only for their quayside whores and for their whiskey. In all his travels, among all the ships' crews, Dad told me, he had met only one sympathetic, artistic soul.

As Dad talked about the quick dawns of the Southern Ocean, a big cargo ship loomed out of the fog, heading west through the Gate, her high steel hull passing not more than forty yards away from us. Her deck lights cast a liquid gleam along her rail. A seaman stood there idly, watching the shore as his ship departed. He saw us in the fog and raised a hand in greeting. We waved back.

Then Dad told again the old story of his captivity aboard a German freighter on which he had booked passage—as a pas-senger this time and not as a seaman—for his crossing of the Indian Ocean toward Africa and eventually Europe. That year was not so very long after World War I, and the German captain had not yet made his peace.

It was summer. The Indian Ocean was hot. The captain stripped my father—this *Eengleesh*—of passenger status and sent him below to chip and paint, to chip and paint, to chip and paint the ceiling of the engine room, all day, day after day. The temperature below the steel deck was so hot, Dad reported, that climbing back almost naked onto the dazzling deck was like stepping into a cold mountain pond.

Dad jumped ship in Port Said and made the rest of his way across the Mediterranean to France in a small coastal freighter. Shortly afterward, he landed at St. John's College, Cambridge University, in the high intellectual pipe-smoke and claret tutorials of F. R. Leavis and of I. A. Richards, each of whom was formative of a then-important new posture of literary criticism called New Criticism. New Criticism advocated close study of the poem itself without any attention paid to the person or the context of the poet. Dad was then, and he remained, deeply skeptical of the efficacy of removing the maker from the made.

I never met Leavis, but during my college years, Ivor and Dorothy Richards would sometimes "cross the herring pond" to teach a course at Harvard, and they would come visit us in New Hampshire. We would all go out into the hills on snowshoes and brew cups of tea over small "barbies" while discussing what should become of poetry in the new world of the 1960s.

Among Dad's pals at Cambridge were William Empson, another New Critic and later a knight, and especially T. H. "Teddy" White, each of whom was beginning to write. Dad and his friends would dash off to hear the latest of the traveling debates between the Christian G. K. Chesterton and the atheist-turned-mystic G. B. Shaw (you could hear every word of Chesterton, even from the back row; Shaw mumbled), or else they would go striding about upon the moors. I loved to imagine my father and Teddy White on windy walks, with mufflers and pipes. I loved this image of the two of them because I loved White's Arthurian fantasy *The Once and Future King,* on which the musical *Camelot* was based.

After a time, Dad's storytelling ceased, and we stood in silence, gazing out across the Pacific toward Dad's old adventure. "And how are you now, Dad?" I asked after a time.

Dad looked at me. We were of the same height by then, he and I, with me perhaps a trifle taller if I flexed my toes. "I should say I am a reasonably happy man."

Not what I had wanted to hear, at all, at all, for I was only just reasonably happy myself.

CHAPTER SEVENTEEN

My first wife and I arrived in Berkeley eighteen months after 1967's "summer of love." We were not ourselves flower children, but we were titillated to have found our way to what, only recently, a breathless media had made famous as the drug and sex capital of the universe. You could wander around the Haight-Ashbury district, eighteen months after "the gathering of the tribes," and observe that the hippie scene was still extant in the way people dressed (or undressed) and the decor of the head shops. But there was beginning to be a grubbiness about it too—its fingernails were getting dirty.

We were New Englanders, my wife and I. What impressed us about the Bay Area were sensual things—the very light dazzled our eyes. The pavement of some streets in Berkeley was painted pink! There were flower baskets hanging everywhere, flowers whose names glided sensually across our tongues as we spoke them. And wine! You could go and watch people make it. You could sit in a garden beside a vineyard, and draw out a cork, and loll in the sunshine, and eat triangles of Roquefort *feuilletés* that your wife had just baked that morning.

My wife and I loved California's physical beauty—the bones of the earth showed through its tan, dry skin. We loved fruit we had never seen before, beautiful as jewels. We loved striding down a trail up in the foothills and stopping to speak intimately with some fellow strider going the other way, until we noticed that no last names were exchanged. A last name points to a past. We striders, it seemed, had no pasts. I was troubled that we should consider ourselves motes and spindrift of the Universal Consciousness, with no actual history of our own.

As much as we delighted in the sensual, we were also impressed with intellectual things. You could wander across the Berkeley campus under the eucalyptus trees—with now and then a whiff of tear gas on the air, for this was, after all, the time of People's Park and its riots—and you could stroll down Telegraph Avenue to Shambhala Books, where you could inhale the mystical incense that burned beside the cash register, and you could dip into volumes on tarot or volumes speculating about the religious consciousness of dolphins. When you were done with such esoterica, you could then leaf through volumes on theosophy, and you could make your way to pages describing the orgies of Aleister Crowley.

Living large!

Then you would stroll farther down Telegraph and wander into Cody's Books, and there you would find volumes about British bohemians, some of whom your dad had met—though, as he told you later, with caution. They had an aura, though, those British Bloomsbury pals, all of them circulating around Leonard and Virginia Woolf. Their photographs in the books were black and white, which was soothingly dated to the eye, and which was unlike the still psychedelically vibrant colors that exploded among the hippies of our own time. Still, these British bohemians espoused free love and communism and pacifism and atheism and freedom from social convention, just as our hippies did.

My wife and I had on our coffee table Bloomsbury memoirs depicting the excitements of the 1930s. She and I were amazed. These bohemians would try anything, at first it seemed.

An example of what they would try was reported to us in literary form in Virginia Woolf's novel *Orlando*. In it, Woolf toys with the eponymous character—who was probably based on her lover Vita Sackville-West. As Sackville-West's son states in his critique of the novel, Woolf "explores Vita, weaves her in and out of the centuries, tosses her from one sex to the other, plays with her, dresses her in furs, lace and emeralds, teases her, flirts with her, drops a veil of mist around her."[2]

Everything was tolerable to the bohemians; especially tolerable was any sort of sex.

However, there was one thing that was apostasy. There was one thing which absolutely they would not tolerate: religious belief.

That particularly dark heresy pierced Virginia Woolf to the quick. When T. S. Eliot converted to the Church of England, Woolf cut him severely. To her sister, Woolf wrote, "I have had a most shameful and distressing interview with poor dear Tom Eliot, who may be called dead to us all from this day forward. He has become an Anglo-Catholic, believes in God and immortality, and goes to church. I was really shocked. A corpse would seem to me more credible than he is. I mean, there's something obscene in a living person sitting by the fire and believing in God."[3]

So sneered this heroine of literary feminists . . . and future suicide.

While fascinated by my exposure to a more lurid sensuality than I had experienced before, I was troubled, too. Those bohemians left their suicides all over the stage, scattered around like the bodies littering the fifth act of a Shakespearean tragedy. All this was very confusing to me. What was I to do with it?

My fundamental belief was that it is *good* when someone discovers that he believes in God. To believe in God one must acknowledge that one has a history and an actuality of one's own.

As a boy, I had not known Eliot well. When he would visit us in Cambridge during his trips back to the States from his adopted England, he was not one of the poets who found it easy to be pals with a child. He and Dad liked each other well enough, I could see that, and Mom once told me that Eliot admired Dad's burning lyrics—because, as she said to me, he was too cerebral to have produced such language himself.

Mostly, I remember that there was laughter around the dining table about Britishisms. Later, when I was older, Mom would remember some of them for me. For example, Eliot once reassured Mom about the timing of a future appointment by saying that he would "just come around and knock you up." Once, Eliot gave me a copy of his thin book of nonsense verse, *Old Possum's Book of Practical Cats*, which I have always enjoyed, coming as it did from a man whose name has become synonymous with esoteric allusions to nearly every element of Western and Eastern language and art and philosophy. But the cats were just funny.

Eliot converted to Anglicanism in 1927. I was pleased to have known him *after* his conversion, not before. In Berkeley, at seminary, I enjoyed stories of those who had gone through a conversion experience, since conversions seemed to me to come from finally discovering who you are. Of course, at seminary I didn't know much about this Jesus guy, but still.

Woolf had sentenced Eliot to literary and social death when he affronted her atheism. But some of Eliot's verse I had found to be thoughtfully religious—"Journey of the Magi," for example.

So I went back and I reread Eliot, and I realized that his next major poem after "The Waste Land" could be said to answer that poem's frightening emptiness of the human condition. "The Hollow Men" could be said to lay out starkly the two existential choices before us humans. This was a new idea to me, and it was exciting. Just as my grade-school teacher had missed the point of Frost's "The Road Not Taken," perhaps critics had missed the bellwether of Eliot's own future that he set before us in "The Hollow Men."

Here are the closing lines of "The Hollow Men"—

This is the way the world ends
This is the way the world ends
This is the way the world ends
Not with a bang but a whimper.

Perhaps the poet who wrote those lines knew in his heart that he had only two roads before him, between which he must choose. Perhaps Eliot stood there—in his yellow wood—and he looked down each road as far as he could, to where they bent in the undergrowth.

One road led to suicide; the other road led to God.

I'm happy that, by the time I knew him, Eliot had taken the one that made all the difference.

I would be surprised if there were one other student at Pacific School of Religion just then who was agonizing as I was agonizing over Eliot and Woolf. But then, that's why my later doctorate is in religion and art and not in theology, or church history, or New Testament exegesis, or Greek.

So many, many were the attractions of the San Francisco Bay Area. As a seminary student I made close study of the history of Western visual and language arts in connection with its religious fundamentals. But beyond that, it was a sunny-skinned and a love-drenched California that my wife and I explored. How, indeed, was very much else to capture my attention when the competition on any given day might include celebrating Buddha's birthday on the slopes of Mount Tamalpais with tambourines, flutes, topless women, and wine?

The poor old Episcopalians didn't stand a chance.

CHAPTER EIGHTEEN

Near the end of his existence, Scott Nearing became a friend of mine. My wife and I began to work for him and for his wife Helen when he was eighty-nine. Scott starved himself to death two weeks after his hundredth birthday. The willpower of the man!

Scott was, and remains, an evangelist of subsistence living, his fame resting on the fortuitous reissuing of his self-published book *Living the Good Life* at the very moment when my generation decided it wanted to go back to the land.

Our friendship was based on Scott's intent to provide my wife and me with agricultural emancipation. We were in California, and Scott and Helen were in Maine, about ten miles from Undercliff. In our VW bug, my wife and I drove across the country about a dozen times, from one pole of our lives to the other. We knew Scott by composting with him, by hauling rocks with him, by building concrete-and-stone walls with him, by thinning scallions with him, by following his instruction on the strategic pruning of young tomato vines. Together, we all ate the plain, vegetarian food that Helen prepared, and we discussed what seemed to Scott to be plainly obvious truths.

Like some Zen master, when he moved, talked, or stayed still, Scott never seemed to be ahead of himself or behind himself—he was always precisely of the moment in which he was.

Scott and I might stand next to each other in the open door of his barn, companionably, neither one of us saying a word, but each one of us sharpening our scythes until the edges were razors, each one of us watching the cumulous summer sky as it darkened over the sea, each one of us eyeing the remaining three acres of hay yet to cut. Then Scott would utter that single guttural chuckle that was his laugh and repeat to me some aphorism that Trotsky had used with him back in the day.

Leon Trotsky!

I was accustomed to Dad knowing important literary names from the past, but here was a different realm in degrees of separation. Standing in Scott's barn door in Maine, I was suddenly two degrees away from Leon Trotsky.

I don't know the circumstances of Scott's acquaintance with Trotsky, but during the 1920s and the early 1930s, when Scott was a socialist and then later a member of the American Communist Party, he was widely read internationally among radicals, and he traveled to the Soviet Union as a voice with an important following. Scott told me that he had thought hard about whether he should stay in the USSR, since it was the one place in the world where a true experiment was being tried regarding equal distribution of capital.

Helen was a water witch, and while Scott and I sharpened our scythes, she would be out near the roses with my wife teaching her how to make clouds disappear by the exercise of her will—for there were three acres of hay yet to cut, and to delay the rain was important. Helen was probably also telling her about her youthful and unsuccessful infatuation in India with the mystic and philosopher Krishnamurti. And the bees would bumble drunkenly in an excess of pollen.

Scott was famous for boasting to us that he had lost his last job in the 1920s. This always got the attention of the young acolytes who traipsed to Scott's farm. Scott had been fired from his position as a professor of economics at the Wharton School of the University of Pennsylvania because he espoused pacifism and socialism. Since then, Scott had survived by speaking, writing, and subsistence farming, first in Vermont and then for twenty years in Maine.

The longer I knew Scott, though, the more I came to suspect that he was too much of an individualist to have thrived in Stalin's workers' paradise. Back in the United States, Scott could live exactly as he wanted to live and have the freedom to say whatever he was pleased to say to whomever he might attract. This was not how Stalin ran things in his own country.

My wife and I loved the deliberativeness of our socialist peasant existence at Scott and Helen's Forest Farm. After four hours of hard physical labor each morning, we would sit in the sun in the alfresco eating area outside Helen's kitchen door, and we would lunch on plain, raw fare, eating from wooden bowls with chopsticks or with rolled-up lettuce leaves as scoops. There were usually some eight or ten fellow travelers along with us. My wife and I were the permanent crew. We had the privilege of intimacy with Scott and Helen, while the passersby often got only dialectic. All the passersby were there to sit at Scott's feet—young people who appeared daily to hear the oracle and to imagine themselves free of silly old capitalism, or at least free of silly old supermarket produce.

We were a cell. Now and then, as we worked the concrete and stone, a dark-colored, very plain sedan would find its way along the back road that led to Forest Farm. The car would squeak to a stop. With its windows rolled up tight, it would remain for about ten minutes. There were always two large, young men in the front seat. Photographs would be taken through the window glass.

Somewhere, in some file in the FBI, I imagine there are photographs of my wife and me, toiling for labor's release. Actually what we were doing was helping to build Scott and Helen's new house. Scott plodded stolidly about his tasks as the agents observed. Helen, more vivacious, made faces at the agents, or she gestured for them to come help us lug some monstrous stone. But the Midwestern farm boys—as we sneered at them—never did come to help. Later, crusty Scott would lecture us about the humorlessness of the American government and about its inevitable collapse.

Ours was a mild experience of the Communist paradise. For us, there were no barricades and no bombs. The sun shone down, and the rose hips reddened, and the lettuces were as big as bushel baskets. Helen was the charmer. She was the salt that enlivened Scott's stew. In time, I came to see Scott as the "poet" of his ideology. He thought poetry of my father's type was without merit and told me so—with its spiritual intent and with its humanistic desire to delve man's fallen condition. Dad's poetry stood contrary to socialist materialism. It was the regularity of Scott's actions, the precision of his pronouncements, and the Zen-like minimalism of his passions that made his life seem to me a created object, almost in an artistic sense. He was no Homer; his life told no high heroic tale. But it did have the neat, small perfection of haiku.

In August of one summer, Scott and Helen offered my wife and me thirty acres of their land—nice land too, with a water view and a gorgeous cedar swamp, filled, as Helen averred, with elves—for a mere $2,500. However, we must agree to live exactly according to Scott's dictates during our first five years. Scott was old, and he wanted his legacy secured. Two couples before us had been offered similar pieces of land and had accepted them. We were to have the third large piece.

My wife and I thought hard about the Nearings' offer. We went and stood in what was to be our own yellow wood. We searched out and found a good house site, high up, with thick forest protection from the northwestern winds, yet open to the warmer south. The gardens would need to be below, but water was available at the house's height—there was a spring—and if we wanted to hear nothing at all except the shriek of an eagle, we could.

Were we truly fit for, and truly committed to, five years of subsistence living? Was our marriage strong enough to stand it? How would we weather the deepest winter months, when there would be very few people available for relief? What if we were to feel a tug from *Reve* one fall, before she was hauled out for the winter?

What if, one fall, when we ought to be stocking carrots and potatoes into the root cellar, we should come into a string of gorgeous days and desire, instead, to cruise? Scott would be against it. Scott and Helen's new house at Forest Farm, the house we helped them build, looks down a cove and out to sea, westward across Penobscot Bay. Scott had never been out on the water, not once, during his twenty years on the coast of Maine. Why should he go out on the water, he questioned me briskly when I asked him about this—his landlocked state which seemed incomprehensible to me. Being out on the water was neither bread labor, since he was not a fisherman, nor was it avocation (writing, lecturing) or even recreation (sitting and thinking, or playing music). Therefore it did not fit in.

One Sunday, I snuck Helen out to Pond Island for a tour—"Don't tell Scott," she begged, only half humorously. This was her first time ever out on the bay in a boat, and there was real anxiety in her voice. At the end of our island ramble, Helen insisted that we must fill the skiff with stones suitable for wall building, so that if Scott should chance to discover our adventure, we would be able to prove that we had been doing bread labor nonetheless.

Now, when my wife's and my workday was done at Forest Farm, most evenings we went home to Undercliff. There, the ethos was artistic and humane, the great yearning was toward the *im*material and where to go in the *Reve* tomorrow, and people enjoyed fun for fun's sake.

The contrast with Forest Farm was too stark. In the end, my wife and I took the road that we took. We declined Scott's offer to join him in the creation of his new subsistence paradise.

.' *   *   *

In time, my wife and I had our degrees, and we were both of us teaching at a Vermont prep school that had (and still has) very close ties with the US Ski Team. For several years, I saw my students racing on TV sometimes more often than I saw them in class, at least during Olympic events.

Later, my wife and I were not married any longer. Our community was tiny, halfway up a ski mountain in what's called Vermont's Northeast Kingdom. It would be awkward for the two of us to remain cheek by jowl. Though I was dreadfully hurt by our divorce, I felt I had more options than she. I resigned from the school so she could remain.

I moved to Boston, roomed with a college pal, drove a cab, acquired seaman's papers, hung around the hiring hall looking for a ship, waited for Vermont to finalize the divorce papers, and wrote as though I were powered by a demon.

But my pal was getting married, so pretty soon my roommate gig would come to an end. I was, of course, having nothing to do with women—forever. Or, well, maybe not *forever* but at least for five years. The good news was that my pal's fiancée had a best friend who was smart and pretty—a sassy Barnard gal. She was just as much roped into the marriage preparation as I was. But that was okay, since everyone knew I was having nothing—*ever*—to do with a woman. So this friend of the bride and I could just enjoy each other's company as we helped with the coming marriage.

That friend's name was Channa. It still is.

CHAPTER NINETEEN

I was in a muddle.

Did I want to become deeply involved with a new woman? No.

Did I want to become deeply involved with Channa? Incredibly—yes.

But what would all that lead to?

I was safer if I said no. I was safer if I held rigidly to my no. I was safer if I controlled everything around me. I was safer if I did not allow anything—and particularly any woman—to penetrate my lone self.

And yet now Channa had a claim on me. Her claim gripped me with extreme strength. Her claim gripped me with extreme strength from a direction I had not, until now, experienced the claim of a woman to come from.

Of course, Channa was beautiful. Of course, Channa was smart. Of course, Channa was funny. Of course, Channa was sassy. Of course—amazingly—Channa even liked to hear me talk. And she was, exotically, a Jew. But it was Channa's character that had a claim on me. She was a woman of granite character, and her rock-solidness astonished me. She knew who she was without agonizing about it.

When her black hair was precisely curled, and she wore her backless dress, and she walked with me into a party, her sparkling eyes, her wide grin, and her loud, infectious laugh were instantly the center of the entertainment. And I—who knew by then that I had the inside track against her other suitors—I could stand back and admire this paragon.

One week, Channa and I went sailing. After a while, we anchored between Maine's Round and McGlathery Islands, and rowed ashore to Round. We each explored the coastline in a different direction. In time, I came around to the island's south end, which was a long slope of granite, against which the waves broke that day with gouts of spray.

When I could see the granite slope, I stopped. Channa was sitting there. She was utterly still. Her knees were up, and her arms were clasped around them, and her back was straight, and her gaze was one thousand miles long. She was as still as Moses might have been when, at long last, he was allowed his one sight of the Promised Land.

I watched Channa's absorption for a time, and then I went and sat beside her on her rock. She acknowledged my presence by the touch of her shoulder against mine, but by no other act—no turning of her face toward me, no speech, no motion, no smile. For perhaps an hour, Channa allowed her profound silence to continue, which relieved me, for we were both by then subsumed entirely within the presence of that for which we both yearned.

Wonderful, that hour.

When the time passed, and when her body language showed that she had returned and was ready to talk, I turned to this beautiful woman, and with my most soulful eyes, I indicated the totality of my love for her by breathing, "Being with you is like being alone."

Instantly, there came that great Channa smile, that great Channa laugh, that great Channa grasping of the whole of the moment, instantly, and getting her comment just right.

"Dikkon, I hope what you meant to say is that being with me is *as good as* being alone."

And of course I had meant *as good as*.

Ever since then, in our private language, *Round Island* has stood for complete joy in the presence of the holy.

Later during that cruise, we were anchored in Southwest Harbor off Mount Desert Island. I was tense and trying not to show it. I had something that my heart was pressuring me to say. That something that my heart was pressuring me to say was a thing that my head was keeping me from saying.

I was a basket case.

We were sitting across from each other in the cockpit. Channa's eyes were lasers and her lips were thin.

"What?"

"Isn't this just beautiful?" I gestured around. "I love this."

"What, Dikkon?"

"Nothing. Just, I love being here with you."

"Dikkon, what?"

I stood up. I stalked to the wheel and rattled it a little. I looked up at the rigging as though to police for a loose line. I took a breath. I put my hands up on the furled mainsail and bent my body forward in an arch. I let out the breath in a whoosh.

I put my hands in my pockets and stalked forward and stepped over the coaming of the forward hatch and stepped down onto the top step of the ladder and turned to face the stern and braced my elbows out on each side of the cabin top.

My eyes caught Channa's. Brighter lasers.

I looked away.

Then I looked back. Then I blurted, "What if I say that I want to marry you?"

Time screeched to a stop. My head hummed. My lungs had squeezed shut. I could scarcely see Channa's eyes through the fog across my own.

"Do you?"

"I don't *know!*"

Coward, my head exploded. *Coward! Coward! Coward!*

Dad and me—each of us a basket case when it comes to marriage proposals!

Nine months later, Channa and I married. The ceremony was held at the Wellesley Inn, a secular setting, though our vows were heard by an Episcopal priest who had originally studied to be a rabbi—so we checked off both boxes for our three living grandmothers.

In the 1970s, we who knew that there are dozens of religions in the world reacted to this fact in opposite ways. Some concluded that since there were so many religions, none of them could be true. Therefore, the sensible thing to do—the enlightened thing—was to set religion aside and to declare for secularism. Others concluded that, since there were so many religions, there must be a truth toward which they were all striving. Therefore, the sensible thing to do—the humble thing—was to declare for God . . . and to await further instruction.

I was a Godian. I believed in God. Channa was an atheist and did not.

Channa and I had enjoyed our honeymoon on Nantucket Island in March, when we got sunburns one day and were snowed in the next. Our second honeymoon came during that summer. Professors of mine in Berkeley had pursued me over the years to come back and to do a doctorate, so I answered their call. Fortunately, Channa's real estate syndication employer in Boston had just opened a San Francisco office, and they agreed to send Channa out there to help get it going.

For our second honeymoon, we drove Channa's grandmother's old Dodge sedan, slowly, across the country. Its enormous backseat was filled with bedding, so at night we alternately slept and drove, while remaining on the highway and knocking off the miles. But during the day we would leave the highway and meander wherever the map intrigued us or where the Lord pointed us to go.

It was a wonderful second honeymoon.

It was about to get even better.

CHAPTER TWENTY

One June day, almost two years after we moved to Berkeley, Channa called the hospital and described a particular event. The nurse responded that Channa had better come in later that evening. I knew everything to do. Everything was already packed. I had run every possible route to Alta Bates hospital at any time of the day, in any traffic condition, in any weather condition. The car was always full of gas; there was always an envelope of cash in the glove compartment in case at that moment we were—ah, broke. We dashed—slowly, because Channa was an elephant and elephants need time to place their feet just so. Twelve hours later, we held our daughter Lena in our arms.

And twelve hours later, Channa knew, absolutely, that God is.

There was nothing to keep us in California. I had finished my coursework and had only the dissertation left to go, and Channa had left her company and begun freelance editing during her pregnancy, which meant work could travel with her. Desperately missing New England weather and greatly burdened by the fact that we had missed the famous blizzard of '78, we decided it was time to bid Berkeley adieu.

We were moving back to Maine!

Camden, Maine, is a pretty, coastal town—into whose harbor I had sailed many times. At that time, Camden was the location of one book publisher and three magazine publishers. Surely, with my skills, I could get work in Camden, and we would live a perfect life.

We arrived in Maine in midsummer and stayed at Undercliff. Daily, I drove the almost two hours, one way, from Undercliff to Camden, looking for work and a place to live. Daily, I returned with neither leads nor success.

Just as desperation was beginning to set in, we happened upon a house we liked, an old Cape Cod with a massive collapsing barn, up above the town, with a view across a lake to a mountain. I went to talk with the director of a local bank whose business was growing and whom I had heard might have a sense of humor. I needed a man with a sense of humor.

Was I married? Yes. Did I have children? Yes. Did I have a job? No. What skills did I have? Editing, writing, building if I needed to. Why should I give you a mortgage? Because you want to, otherwise you wouldn't be talking to me. That cracked him up. He looked me up and down. Well, he said, you look to me like a man who can support his family. Okay, I'll give you that mortgage.

A day or two later, one of the restaurants called. You still available? Yes. Our chef just quit. Can you start tonight? Sure.

So I cooked and wrote; Channa waitressed and edited. Lena sat bundled up next to the woodstove in the living room fascinated by the fast talking of our friends at our parties. My first novel, *On the Verge*, was published, and the same publisher bought my second novel, *Paradise*, a vigorous nautical and theological adventure set in the sixth century AD. And somehow, despite the fact that I came home from work at midnight stinking of garlic and shrimp, Channa was pregnant again.

Then suddenly, with no warning, the man who owned the restaurant tired of it and closed it. The only compensation the other chef and I received was the right to empty the walk-in refrigerator of anything stored there and to take it home for our personal use. So—though Channa and I were back to being broke—for several months we fed our family (and lots of our friends) with beef tenderloins, extra-colossal shrimp, hand-trimmed smoked hams, and veal medallions, and I could whip up *coquilles Saint-Jacques* using perfect, individually flash-frozen, deep-ocean scallops that were the best to be found north of Boston.

About two months after the restaurant closed, the phone rang. It was the man who had chaired my doctoral committee in Berkeley. He had just accepted a new position as president of Hartford Seminary in Connecticut, and he wanted to know if I would be available to move to Hartford right away to take a faculty-level position administering the seminary's library, archives, and bookstore while advising doctoral candidates. He named a salary that included faculty housing and sounded astounding to an out-of-work chef who had a toddler and a pregnant wife—now a *very* pregnant wife.

Hmmm, I was planning to change the oil in the car, but, well, let me think . . .

So we rented out our house in Camden, on the cool coast of Maine, and we arrived in sweltering Hartford.

My first assignment was to turn around the seminary's

moribund bookstore by the end of the summer—with the budget necessary to do so, as approved by the board. As it happened, one of the members of the board was Katharine Hepburn's sister, and as we got to know her—just a little—it was fascinating to hear her speaking in one room of our house when we were in another. She and her sister had exactly the same intonation. I would refill the appetizer tray while listening to the movie star's voice in the other room and then come back expecting to pass the crackers to Spencer Tracy.

Two weeks after we arrived in Connecticut, our son James was born, two days after Lena's second birthday.

James, that fine son, was the easiest of Channa's births. By then, Channa knew all about having babies. She's a quick study, my wife. She's also generously interested in the welfare of those around her. What with the tension of the move at the height of her pregnancy, Channa had been very conscious of pain—of *my* pain, that is. I'd hurt my back lugging stuff. So there she was, this hugely pregnant woman, almost fully dilated and with regular, cramping contractions, being wheeled into the birthing room with her husband holding her hand.

Channa turned to the nurse. "Do you have any aspirin?"

The nurse looked at her with an amused smile. "Honey, I don't think that's going to help."

Channa burst out laughing. "No, not for me. It's for him."

Just a few pushes later, there he was: James—congenial from the first, loyal, affectionate, tender, smart, a teaser. We brought James home, and we showed him to Lena in his bassinette. Lena was delighted with her new toy.

So there we were—two young 'uns, a real job for me that could lead to a career, one novel published and another—sold!—nearing completion. It almost felt as though I was actually, finally, for once in my life, *doing* something.

Then . . .

One day, when Lena was five and was lying in our hammock with me, she injected her own theology into what was still our family's Godianity. The day was windy and cold. It was late autumn. Lena and I enjoyed our hammock swing. Then she, normally an eager chatterer, fell silent.

After a bit, she said, "Daddy, I can tell there's a God."

This enchanted me. "How, sweetie?"

"See the leaves?" She gestured at the tree above us. "You can't see the wind, but it's there. You can't see God . . ." She hesitated.

"But you know He's there?" I prompted.

"Yes," she nodded. "He makes people move, like the leaves."

Then she pondered some more and snuggled against me and whispered, "And God can be cold sometimes too."

Thus, the daughter of a Godian!

Lena had more on her mind. My doctorate had enriched our family with the greatness of human artistic striving in order to touch the divine (not to mention, it had given me my job), but Lena had a question, and her question was pointed.

"Daddy, what do we believe?"

Plunk!

Lena had tossed a stone into my serene religious pond.

I did not like it that I could not answer her question.

Despite Channa's rich Jewish heritage—her great-grandfather had been an Orthodox rabbi—and my seminary education, really, Channa and I knew very little about any actual religion, be it Judaism or Christianity—or any other kind of religion, including the religious consciousness of dolphins. Of course, I had two master's degrees and a PhD and could talk quite a lot about the Bible and the paintings and novels that came from its witness, but what good did that do when it came down to actually believing something?

So Channa took a comparative religion course at the seminary, and I, being an academic, thought and thought.

Godianity was out. That was final. It would be either Christianity or Judaism.

I did not *get it* about Jesus, so Jesus and the religion about Him were out. On the other hand, I loved the humanity, the clarity, the justice, and the exuberance of the Hebrew Bible—which is such a great human story—in which Yahweh has our best interests at heart, even when His people refuse to recognize that it is so.

Okay, then. Resolved: the children will be raised as Jews.

This would be Channa's deal, since she was already Jewish, and the children, therefore, were Jewish too. I would be a supportive husband and father, and a Godian dropout.

In Channa's efficient way, she got busy. She learned of a *Havarah* in our town (an informal gathering of Jews for prayer and learning, usually not led by a rabbi). Channa and I began to attend, and Lena and James went to the Sunday school along with a changing population of other young Jewish hopefuls.

One day, Lena brought home a tiny twist of paper from Sunday school, with notes written in her own hand. She asked Channa, "Can we do this on Friday?"

This was to say a prayer, to light candles, to eat a special sort of bread, and to drink a sip of wine. Grape juice would be okay for the children. Very likely, Lena also had with her a recipe for the special bread, called challah, the making of which, with one's children, would be a fine, ethnic thing to do before the Friday dinner.

I was suspicious about this prayer: What words were creeping into my household? Hmm. Let's see. The prayer on the paper was written in Hebrew but was conveniently translated into simple English. The prayer was addressed to God, who was identified as the Creator of the Universe. So far, so good. The rest of the prayer thanked Him for the light from the candle and for the bread and the wine.

All right, I thought. *I can accept that; no problem.* So that Friday night, at supper, for the first time, awkwardly, our family celebrated Shabbat.

Here's what I, the academic, thought: after all, it is *right* for my wife and my children to want firmness of identity, and if Jesus isn't in my personal picture, then there is nothing more glorious and meaningful than the life of a Jew, one of God's own chosen covenant people, heirs to a tradition of nearly four thousand years, intense students of the Hebrew Bible.

To thank the Creator of the Universe for the gifts of light, and of food, and of drink, I thought, need not offend me, the ex-Godian. But what I did not know on that first Shabbat night is that such prayers would challenge mere ex-Godianity, and that they would win.

Religious ceremonies exert their power on those who live them. Prayers work.

When you pray to God, God notices you. When God notices you, you sense it, and you yearn to please Him more. You yearn to please Him by praying harder, by welcoming Shabbat more intensely, as the bridegroom welcomes the bride (a frequently used Jewish metaphor for the act of welcoming Shabbat). You become more ceremonious in your Shabbat preparation, more thorough, more delighted. You long for Friday evening as you never did before. You study God's language and find that you are praying in what had been to you a foreign tongue, but is His own.

On Friday evening, everyone knows that table conversation is going to be about God, and about Shabbat, and about why we are thus remembering Him. There will be stories about the past. There will be laughter. That evening, the father and the mother know, their family will be blessed to do what Jewish families have done for centuries, upon centuries, upon centuries, every Friday evening, as the years have rolled along in their diurnal way. And when dinner is over, the children will be tucked into bed, secure in the certainty that they and their family are integral to something greater than themselves, and, by that miracle, that they have identity, that they have purpose, that they are safe.

What I did not understand that first awkward night was that, as Channa and I stumbled through our first Shabbat prayers, God already knew us as the man and the woman He had planned for us to become. Certainly He knew that I would convert to Judaism, though it took His whispered invitation to me during Yom Kippur service a few years later to start that process. He knew that Channa and I would be deep appreciators of His gift to His chosen people, and that we would share that appreciation with our children. God also knew—though it would have astonished us—that more than twenty years later, Channa and I would become joyful acceptors of something else as well.

But first, it was too hot in Connecticut.

CHAPTER TWENTY-ONE

"And there," I concluded my story, "is the witch's leg!"

I pulled the car over in Bucksport, Maine, so that Lena and James could stare at the tall granite grave marker on which there is an indelible mark in the shape of a woman's leg from knee to toe, under the last name of the man who is buried there, Colonel Jonathan Buck.

"The leg! The leg will follow you to your grave!"

This is what was shrieked at Buck by the deformed son of a witch who was burned to death in 1719 under Buck's authority. As the witch was burning, her lower leg rolled free and lay there before the horrified spectators.

Cursed as a witch and driven from town, living in a hovel with her adult son, nevertheless this woman had been hauled before the town elders when things turned bad for the townspeople. The witch claimed innocence, but *someone* must have caused the bad times, and who among the town's population was the obvious culprit?

Burn her they must, and burn her they did.

Later, at his own allotted time, Colonel Buck died, covered with honors and much admired by the town. He was buried in the cemetery. Years later, the town set up a monument in his memory, the very one at which Lena and James were staring. And what do you suppose happened? One day, townspeople saw that a stain *in the form of a woman's leg* had appeared on the grave. Horrified, they remembered the curse, and they scrubbed and they scraped and they chipped. But the stain remained!

In fact, the monument has been replaced twice—and the same stain keeps appearing!

My children were thrilled and shivery, all at once. And I was pleased—and Channa grinned at me conspiratorially—because I had kept them amused as I told my unfolding story (with much greater detail than here) during the last hour of the drive toward Undercliff, and I had timed my final line of the story to the very moment when we were abreast the monument itself.

The curtain fell. The wide eyes of my two children were applause enough. Now: only forty minutes to go.

To Undercliff!

We were almost home.

* * *

After every dinner at Undercliff, my father settled back in his chair at the end of the dining table, while the rest of us scattered to couches or to rockers or to the floor before the fire. Dad would set the evening's talk agenda, to get the flow going, by throwing out a provocative question. Dad cared little for any softening verbal caress; with his questions, he was direct and confrontational. Any guest might be challenged by a question unblemished by nuance.

On this particular evening, a few days after our arrival, Dad was challenging a summering lawyer. "You're a Catholic. How can the Pope be infallible, Craig? How can any man be infallible?"

"Dick, I don't know."

"But that's what you Catholics say. There's been a decree, or a bull, or whatever you call it."

"Well, there needs to be a final authority. . . ."

"But not *a man* as the authority. It's absurd."

"It's about faith and morals, Dick. When the Pope speaks ex cathedra, he *can't* speak falsely. It's impossible. When speaking ex cathedra, the Pope is imbued by the Holy Ghost, and so—"

"But then he's not a man!"

"Of course, he's a man, Dick. What else would he be?"

"Not if he's imbued with the Holy Spirit. That makes him a god."

"No it doesn't. What about the apostles, at Pentecost? They were men. They were imbued. They weren't gods."

"When the Holy Spirit is imbuing an apostle," Dad opined with finality, "he's not a man at that moment. He's become some kind of a god." My father looked around the room, gathering our eyes. "What do you others think?"

Dad found me with his eyes, wanting my support. "Dikkon, you're the theologian." Then he turned back to Craig. "But is that really what they teach you? Tell us. You're off to your church every Sunday."

Craig laughed; he was a sailor. In summer, when the boats swung to their moorings out front, cruising was the holy activity of any day, be that day Sunday or otherwise. "No church for me. My wife goes."

"So!" Dad laughed. "You see, you *are* human, after all! And that's why you, anyway, can't be infallible, and that means the Pope can't be infallible either. The very idea is absurd! Only God is infallible, and He's not around to let us know all about it. We're all sinners here under the sun. Devil and angel." He looked around to see if anyone would pick this up. "Devil and angel, that's what I say."

Other random talk had begun and now meandered around the room. Dad's devil-and-angel diagnosis didn't raise an eyebrow.

I could have challenged Dad on his screwball theology, but I was too annoyed to bother. He would only shake off my corrections in his grandiose way. Being a poet, he was accustomed to excusing his own errors.

Mom, back from cleaning in the kitchen, circulated with the coffeepot. "Oh, Richie," she said, "nobody cares."

But Dad wasn't done setting the conversational scene, and he tried one more shot.

"You!" He gestured with the stem of his pipe at a visiting young woman, a writer whose new book about the war between the sexes was high on the bestseller lists right then. She was dressed very provocatively. All the men were pretending not to notice; the women were not so pretending.

"You're a woman," Dad said, unnecessarily. "Why can't two women get along?"

"What do you mean, Dick—women getting along?" She was pretty, and she winked.

"Oh, I don't mean it *that way*." Dad was having fun. "Ha-ha!"

"Then tell me, Dick, just what kind of 'women getting along' are you thinking about? I want to know."

Mom, warningly, while standing in the kitchen door: "Richie."

Dad looked at Mom. With the coffeepot in her hand and a dish towel over one shoulder, she had a cautionary eye on her husband. Dad spread out his arms innocently. "What I mean is, you never see a woman just being pals with another woman. There's always something else going on, some emotion." He turned to the larger group. "Isn't that what you find too? What's that song, Betty, 'Why can't a woman be more like a man?' How's that go?"

Instead of answering, Mom turned to an old Cold Warrior and asked him why the situation in Madagascar was so toxic just now.

Dad did not mind. All he had been trying to do was to stir the pot, to get things going, and anyway he was continuing to talk with the sex author and was enjoying her flirtation.

I sat on the old daybed in the corner next to Channa. Lena was on the floor by our knees, fascinated by the talk. James was cuddled next to Channa with his important cloth against his face, half asleep.

My annoyance at Dad's inaccurate theological balderdash was fading. Why should I care? Wasn't I meandering closer to a Jewish life? What did I care about fine points of Catholic doctrine or about Dad's imputation of godliness to men? Besides, really, I was just then drifting, sun dazed from hours on the boat and from weeks and weeks of trying to wrestle my third novel out of its bloat.

My drift was interrupted by the sex author leaning over to me and asking, "Dikkon, is it true that Dylan Thomas told you bedtime stories?"

"What? Yes. Yes, sure."

"How extraordinary! Tell me everything."

Channa had watched the woman come close, and so she had placed her hand on my knee.

Before I could respond, Grandmother levered herself up from her rocker by the fire, "Well, my dears, I must love you and leave you."

Dad picked up a flashlight and said, "I'll light you out, Mother B."

At that moment, a poet from Florida pushed in through the door, having driven all the way. "Dick! Betty! You asked us to come visit you. Well, here we are! Here we are! And we've brought these two pies."

Hurrah!

The party shuffled companionably sideways, as birds do when a new member slides down the sky to land on their ridge-line and to preen among them.

"You're Dikkon!" the poet cried, grabbing me off the daybed for a hug. "I've read your new novel. I loved it—sea action and all that religious power. Great stuff. Great."

"Thank you. It was fun to—"

"Great. Just great." And he was gone.

Channa gave me a sympathetic look.

I grimaced. I looked around the room, and suddenly I couldn't stand to be in it any longer. I pulled away and slipped outside. I shut the door on the new poet and on the old talk. It was dark outside, and the wind had diminished off the sea.

My book?

My book?

Is there one single word in there that is about *my* book?

This is my father's world, and I can't get away from it. There's no room left!

Why was it so hard for me to be something—of my own?

As soon as I thought I was something, I wasn't. I thought I was a Godian, and then I wasn't. I thought I was a novelist, and then I couldn't finish the third one. I thought I was an academic, but I disliked academic politics and self-conceit. I thought I was a man who would speak up to save a little girl, and then I wasn't. I thought I was a man who could charm his way out of marital jail, and then I wasn't.

Channa stepped out of the house and found me on the beach. Her arm went through mine. "Are you okay?"

"Let's just put the children to bed, and go to bed ourselves, and not care."

"Shouldn't we say good night?"

I sighed. "I will. You round up the kids."

Channa repeated, "But are you okay?"

"It is what it is."

We returned to the cottage, which was warm with the fire and the talk. Channa rounded up the children and led them away.

Dad, the famous lyricist, infuriatingly doltish when it came to the play of human emotion around him—for example, my emotions—tried to engage me with the Florida poet, whom I was determined to dislike. And as I usually did, I allowed myself to be drawn back into Dad's conversation. He was my father, after all. I didn't get away until much time had passed.

When I slid into bed, Channa was already asleep.

Dikkon, the Son of the Poet.

CHAPTER TWENTY-TWO

Channa's third pregnancy was different. The baby was in a breech position, and though attempts were made to position the little person properly, none of them worked.

It was early December in Connecticut, and Lena and James did not yet have winter boots. One day I was at work, and Channa called. "The contractions are getting closer and more regular."

"I'll come home."

When I reached home, the contractions had slowed down, but we still didn't have the boots. Channa had a new plan. She was experienced at giving birth, and we still had the boots on our to-do list before the baby came. We had called the friends with whom Lena and James were to stay in case this was indeed the day; now we called them back and told them the baby wasn't on the way after all. We loaded the kids into the car and drove through heavy rain to the Sears at Corbin's Corner, which is about as far from Hartford Hospital as you can get and still be in the United States. It was early afternoon.

Apparently, every other child in the state of Connecticut had not yet gotten boots that year either. Sears was mobbed with anxious mothers and with dozens of children shrieking and running around the shoe department. Three frazzled salesladies did the best they could. We got Lena done—pink boots for her. We were working on James—and not pink boots by any means.

"Dikkon, it's starting again."

"How close?"

"Very close." She had to sit down. I became even busier than I had been.

Hartford Hospital was miles away. Heavy rain; rush hour; one more pair of boots to buy; keep the kids calm but engage their help.

Bless those two little wonderful humans—they were dreams of assistance to their mother and to me.

My years of cab driving helped—*just get there, it doesn't matter how*. We swung by the house of the friends who were to watch Lena and James. No one was home. "We wait," Channa moaned, clamping an iron grip on my arm. "Five minutes." At minute four, the husband arrived home.

Off we go—fast!

Make shortcuts—even where there isn't one, *create* one!

Hope that a cop will pull us over; get his lights and siren ahead of us.

Go, go, go!

Pull with a screech into Emergency. Nurse pulls open passenger door. "My wife," I shout, "having a baby." But she can see that, and the gurney is there, and Channa is swept into the hospital. I burn to the parking area, brake hard, dash back.

Nurses point me the way to go. I arrive panting at the door of Emergency.

"You can't go in."

"What do you mean?"

"You can't go in; it's too late."

"What do you mean, it's too late! I'm her husband!"

"Just wait here, sir. Just wait."

Sam was born eight minutes after I screeched to a stop at Emergency. In fact, his hand was already born by the time Channa was prepped for an emergency C-section. And then he was there.

A while later, I was allowed to go in. There was Channa, dear Channa, out cold—but fine.

I looked around frantically. No baby.

"You have a son, sir. He's healthy. There's something I need to talk with you about."

"Where is he? What did you say? Did you say something?"

"We're taking a look at him, sir. There's something I need to talk with you about."

"Is something . . . wrong?"

"Let's go into this room over here." When there, "Please sit down, sir. There's something I need to talk to you about."

Since then, often in my heart, I have blessed that doctor for what he did for me that day. I didn't even know what Down syndrome meant. I'd heard of it, but what was it? He walked me through it with infinite patience, clarity, and calmness. The hospital would do some blood tests, of course, but they were virtually certain that Sam had Down's.

Then I went to see my son. The room was dim. Channa was still out cold but expected back soon. Sam was wrapped in a soft blanket close beside her. I had been told that I could hold him, so I did—my new son!

Sam was asleep. I undressed him. Yes, I could see that his chest narrowed near its top. Yes, I could see that his ears were a little low on the sides of his head. Yes, I could feel that his limbs were a little slacker than I should have expected in a newborn. But he felt soft and smooth like a newborn, he smelled like a newborn, he slept deeply as a newborn will when it is full and clean and warm and safe. He was my son.

I sat in a rocker in that dim room and nuzzled him and whispered to him and said hello. I told him that I loved him. He and I sat there for about a half hour before Channa stirred.

I put Sam down at her side and leaned over. Her eyes opened. A soft, tired smile was there. "Hi," she said.

I moved her hand so it touched Sam's head. "That's our son."

"Oh, how nice."

"I love you."

"I love you, too."

"There's something I need to talk with you about."

"That's nice, dear," and she was gone.

About twenty minutes later, Channa emerged into consciousness again. The same thing happened. "There's something I need to talk with you about."

"That's nice, dear," and she was gone again.

And a third time. "That's nice, dear." And gone.

The fourth time when Channa came into consciousness, she was there to stay. This time she was able to look down at Sam and stroke his head. "Oh, how beautiful," she said.

"There's something I need to talk with you about."

"Yes?"

"The doctor thinks Sam has—Down syndrome."

I had spent more than an hour with Sam, just being there, without particular thought, just feeling contented to hold my new son. I suppose that God had just caromed our lives off in an unexpected direction, but I was not thinking about that.

Channa stroked Sam's head for a minute or so. Then she looked at me with that deep, human, gestative wisdom that many women have, and which I don't.

"We know what we've lost. We don't know what we've gained."

CHAPTER TWENTY-THREE

Immediately, we were bombarded by experts—starting at the top.

On Sam's second day of life, none other than Dr. Robert M. Greenstein, the head of genetics at the University of Connecticut, came to see us. He had a research interest in Down syndrome and in human genetic mutations of any sort. He provided both wise and patient counsel and visited several times. We had easy access to him later, when we needed further information.

Various state social-service organizations came to assist and advise us. They would be the ones who would help us with home care while we adjusted. The father of a friend of Lena's, who was an obstetrician whose specialty was high-risk pregnancies, made himself available (while chiding me for targeting Hartford Hospital on boot day, when his own hospital was just a few short miles in the other direction).

And we had an expert of another kind as well—Channa's best friend came on the second day, with a bottle of champagne, and they cried.

Lena and James were delighted by their new brother, who was just an ordinary baby to them. Channa and I were delighted as well—for one thing, Sam slept through the night, contentedly, from the first night he was home.

Having been father to a newborn twice before, I had expected to be busy and to be tired after the new baby was born, but I had not expected another thing: the expert intrusions into our house—helpful, but intrusions nonetheless. There was one other thing I had not expected. Every grandparent knows how to react to the telephone call from the city where their son or their daughter lives at the time when the new baby is due. "It's a boy!" "It's a girl!"

"Yay!"

I encountered an extra responsibility: the responsibility to lead, and to teach.

"Dad, Mom, it's a boy! Samuel Dryden Eberhart!"

"Yay!"

"Earlier today."

"And Channa's okay?"

"Yes. It was a cesarean, but she's fine."

"And how is darling little Samuel?"

"He's fine—ten fingers, ten toes. But, well, the doctor says he might have Down syndrome."

"Oh."

Here's where the leading, the teaching, began. Sam—Channa and I agreed—was simply one more of our children, all of them of the same status, neither higher nor lower; each of them was equal in the sight of God, who had blessed us by providing them to us in the first place, that we should raise them.

Over time, we determined that we would not become activists at raising a child with Down syndrome. Of course, we would become knowledgeable about Sam's condition and would adjust our ways as required, but we would continue in our objective of raising children who are as different from one another as are random wildflowers in a meadow.

I was certain that I had Lena and James all figured out. Lena was six, and I knew for certain that she would be an actress. Just look at her and at the way she interacted with people around her. An actress, for sure. James was four, and I knew for certain that he would be an engineer. Just look at him and at the way he interacted with mechanical things around him. An engineer, for sure.

However, the Down syndrome experts made me furious. I quizzed them hard every time they came to our house. They gave me the same answer every time, and their answer frustrated me.

Yes, we were blessed that Sam did not have the heart problem or the digestive obstruction that sometimes characterizes babies with Down's. But what would Sam be doing when he was four? What would Sam be doing when he was six? The experts said they did not know. What about puberty? They said they did not know.

Well, *of course* they knew! They were *experts*, weren't they? I was Sam's *father*, and I *needed* to know.

What would Sam be doing when he was ten? What would Sam be doing when he was fifteen? What would Sam be doing *then*? I insisted to know.

I had Lena and James all figured out. I needed to figure Sam out too, and the experts—the *experts*—wouldn't help me.

Fie on them!

It took three months for Sam to teach me the first thing that Sam taught me. It took three months of hearing from the experts that they did not know what Sam would be doing at any future time, and that I would need, simply, to wait to find out.

It took three months for me to calm down and to realize that, regarding Sam, there truly was no way to know.

It came into my head, thinking about my father, and about being a father, and about all that stuff, that sometimes fathers annoy their children because the fathers get it all wrong. I remembered the time when Dad told Marie Rexroth that I had moved to California to get a master's in theology. Wrong. Also, Dad had it in his head that I don't drink alcohol. Wrong. Where Dad had gotten that idea, I don't know. But I do enjoy the true, the blushful Hippocrene, as Keats gracefully terms the juice. I just never liked it poured out as sluggingly as Dad poured his own.

Funny, how fathers can get it all wrong sometimes.

Lena the actress . . .

James the engineer . . .

Oh! Wait!

Take a deep breath, Dikkon—thank you, Sam.

Dear Sam, it took you only three months. I'd been a father for six years. It took you only three months, Sam, to make me a wiser father. So I backed off on the actress and the engineer bit. I had no business tying my children down in my mind at their tender ages of six and four—and of three months.

CHAPTER TWENTY-FOUR

During Channa's and my years with young children, we were tugged in a direction opposite from the secular progressive direction that invited many around us. This was especially true as Judaism became ever more fully the definition of our relationship with the world around us and with the world's ideas.

Channa was reconnecting with the Judaism of her extended family, and I was trying to work my way out of intellectual limbo. Both of us took Judaism—it was Reform Judaism that we practiced—seriously. There was a great deal to learn. Judaism is a religion of law, and we strove to understand what Yahweh meant by His Ten Commandments and by His Holiness Code recorded in Leviticus.

Our lives confused us, as did our sins—though I did not term our sins *sins* at that time. That was too accusatory a term. We were not happy with our unhappiness when it erupted. We fought, which exhausted us. We were too, too busy. Rarely was there time for deep theological probing. Rarely, it seemed, was there time for anything at all except for the next frantic trip in the minivan to catch up with what ought to have been finished hours before.

Despite that, though, Channa was pregnant once more. We were no longer Godians, we were not quite yet Jews—but we certainly were repeatable Life-ians.

This time, the birth would be in March, so the need to buy winter boots would not be a problem. Having moved since Sam's birth, we were closer to Hartford Hospital than before. The caretakers for the three children, when the moment came, would come to us, not the other way around. Lena and James were now old enough to understand (and to applaud) that for survival, really, all children actually need is peanut-butter-and-jelly sandwiches.

One day, while sitting on the living room couch, suddenly Channa said, "Dikkon, now."

No rain, no rush hour, not even any lugging of children. What could possibly go wrong?

Oh! The Saint Patrick's Day parade!

Half of the city of Hartford was marching across our route and inserting itself between us and the hospital.

I pressed forward into the throng anyway, honking my horn and getting the most astonished and furious looks from the people in my way. I kept pointing at Channa's belly, but no one bothered to look at her, they just excoriated me.

"Hurry, Dikkon. They're closer. Please hurry."

I crawled.

"Dikkon . . ."

Now I was up against a solid wall of parade watchers, unable to move at all. I just leaned on the horn. Within a minute a livid cop bulled his way through the crowd toward me. "What the—" he was shouting.

I leaned out the window and bellowed back while stabbing my finger across the parade route. "My wife! Baby! Hospital!"

Then we had a wonderful experience. Suddenly, half a dozen policemen were there, urgently clearing the standers away, and then dashing out into the middle of the parade and bringing the entire extravaganza to a halt. Grinning from ear to ear, I drove across the parade route. Some people realized what was happening—now they noticed Channa as she smiled at them and groaned and smiled at them some more—and a cheer went up, and we were celebrated by Hartfordians as we broke free from the parade on its other side and dashed down the street to where we were presented with our next gift from God, a lovely girl, Rosalind—the only one of our children with Channa's black-haired coloring.

CHAPTER TWENTY-FIVE

My mother and I shared the same sense of humor. She was always able to see the funny side of things.

This applied to the genuinely funny moments but also to the unhappy times of life. If she was in the middle of an unhappy time, when the burden was heavy, still she would have flashes of wit—partly, I think, because she was able to distance herself from the problem and to see in the problem what she would call the absurdity of man's estate.

In her later years, the drugs my mother took to control her epilepsy wore her down. Physically, she became frailer. Mentally, she became less able—but her incapacity came and went. Sometimes it was hard for her to order a thought and to reproduce it in voice; sometimes not.

It distressed me and my family when we visited Mom and found her not herself. For me, it was a greater distress to find Mom not herself than to find Dad so. The self my mother had always expressed was intensely interactive, curious, responsive, insightful, and funny. When that self was absent, I experienced loss. On the other hand, when Dad's mental light was dim, he at least showed himself familiarly as the silent, contemplative, poet father. I could sit with him for hours, saying nothing, knowing he was content, feeling content myself, while having no more complex experience of him than his physical presence.

Once, when Dad was ninety-five, he came out of one such silence and asked me a question Mom would never have thought to ask, its entire thought process being so unlike her: "Do you think I should live to be one hundred?"

"Do you want to?"

"I don't know."

I laughed. "Then I don't either."

"Everyone else here—" Dad was referring to his retirement community—"everyone else is dying of something, and I'm not."

"I think you should do what you want to do."

Then came a flash of my father's humor. Looking me in the eye, he said, "I wonder what that is."

My mother was a realist, involved intensely and gratefully in the midst of life. The greatest times in my mother's life, as she told me, were when she and my father were young and *doing something* in the poetry world, and when Gretchen and I were young and she and my father were *doing something* to raise their children into decent adults.

Mom bustled and sang around the house and loved her life as Gretchen and I grew. Certainly, she and Dad fought mightily sometimes—as she attested, "All married fights are about money, sex, or children"—because she cared very much. After she became ill, she fought just as mightily to keep epilepsy from hobbling her or those around her. Mom would not allow herself to be a burden.

A curious thing attested to the affinity of awareness between Mom and me. Mom suffered from petit mal seizures at unexpected times. The seizures generally lasted about ninety seconds, during which, if she were standing, she might collapse or she might just brace herself upright by placing her hand on something solid—for example, dangerously, on a red-hot stove burner. She would come slowly out of the seizure, then, as though waking from a very deep unconsciousness, and she would be ashamed that she might have discomfited those around her.

The curious thing was this. If I was standing within about eight feet of my mother or closer, and if there was no other person between us, and if a seizure was about to start, in my head there would come a buzzing sensation that filled my being. Once I learned that this sensation presaged a seizure, I would have time to lead her to a seat before the seizure began. I do not know why this sensation occurred, and I have not experienced it in any other situation.

Dad and Gretchen bore the worst of Mom's illness.

Dad was anguished for Mom that the condition should exist at all. But Dad thought both emotionally and legendarily. What did epilepsy *mean*? I can hear my mother saying, "Oh, Richie, it doesn't mean anything. It's just life. The only thing it means is that you have to drive me everywhere, and I can never drive myself. That's more trouble for me than it is for you." But Dad would not be satisfied with this dismissiveness, and he would press everyone to learn what epilepsy meant.

Further, Dad was both squeamish around illness and hypochondriacal at the same time. I think this is the deeper reason why Dad never visited Ezra Pound in prison in the early 1950s when many of his pals were urging him to do so. Frost, Eliot, Wilbur, Cummings, and many others in the literary establishment urgently solicited Dad's support in their effort to get Pound released from prison. But Dad declined. Certainly, he hated Pound's politics and considered him traitorous—the man had broadcast fascist polemics for the Mussolini government over Radio Rome during the middle years of World War II. Yet Dad might at least have gone to visit the man, for his poetry, if not to align his name with Pound's. After all, the war was over.

One time when I was in college and mad at Dad, that's how I attacked him. "At least for *The Cantos*! You could have gone to see Pound for *The Cantos*. You love *The Cantos*."

"I just couldn't."

"But why not?"

"He was a fool."

"Okay, I get it about his politics. But can't you separate the man from his work?"

"What are you, a New Criticism man?"

"I just want to know why you couldn't go see Pound."

"We're all of us of a piece, Dikkon. That's what we are. I couldn't go see Pound because I couldn't go see Pound."

Something of the same happened when Frost was dying. I never met Pound, although—especially when I was a college guy—I should have liked to meet him (he and I share a birthday, October 30). But I knew and very much liked Frost.

Mom urged Dad to go, but Dad was scared. "He won't be Robert."

"But he *is* Robert. Oh, Richie, you must."

"I just can't."

"You may never see him again."

And Dad was flummoxed. I was sad about the whole event, sad that Frost was dying, and sad that Dad was unmanned. That about death which fascinated Dad also appalled him. He was like Lear sometimes on the heath.

Ah, life, how canst thou?

Gretchen had a hard time of Mom's illness because it impacted her adolescence as it did not impact mine. During the years when I was at prep school and at college, I was out of the house. During those same years, Gretchen was the only child at home. These were her teen years, when a girl likes to have her mother available for advice and counsel (or to be ignored, as the mood may take her), but during this time, Gretchen needed to keep a watchful eye on her mother in case she should have a seizure. Gretchen has told me that hers was not a hovering sort of experience, exactly, but Mom's illness did live in the house and needed to be attended to—like art.

Mom busied herself with political and community concerns, and now and then she would go niece-hopping, as she called it. She would take off from home and bounce by plane across the country, visiting nieces and godchildren and old college or poetry friends.

Mom was *involved*. She wrote thousands of letters by pencil in her upright script, and they went on and on—one could hear her voice in the sentences—even going sideways or upside down around the margins of the page. She bicycled around Hanover and knew everyone she met. If I was to drive her to the grocery store to buy milk and eggs—which shopping trip ought to have occupied thirty minutes—we returned two hours later because every person we met in the grocery aisle was a friend to be caught up on. She and our next-door neighbor Jean gardened next to each other, each in her own patch, and they solved the problems of the world as they weeded.

I am grateful for the last time I saw my mother alive. She and Dad were living in their retirement community. She had broken her hip and was recuperating from the break itself but deteriorating more in terms of her verbal articulation, and she used a wheelchair. Gretchen's and my family and close friends threw a party for Mom and Dad at Gretchen's lovely home about twenty miles from Hanover. The party went well, and there was much jollity, but I, and I think everyone else, was aware of what a struggle it was for my mother to rise above her physical ailments to participate.

When it was time to take Mom and Dad back to their retirement community, because Mom was unable to walk and the stairs were awkward with the wheelchair, I carried Mom out to the car. She was not heavy. I maneuvered her through doorways, down stairs, and onto the seat of the car. I got her settled and stood back, holding the door open. Her eyes met and held mine. Though she could scarcely speak, her eyes expressed profound intelligence and conscious humor at how absurd all this physical incapacity was. How silly, she seemed to be saying—how silly that she should be so isolated from her children and her grandchildren . . . and what a comedy was life!

I am grateful for that moment, my last sight of my mother alive. The moment left me with the comforting supposition that perhaps her spirit was exactly as it had always been, though we were all aware that the house in which her spirit lived was in poor repair.

Mom died at age eighty, in 1994. It's been twenty years, yet hardly a month goes by when I don't think, regarding something absurd, *Mom would like that.*

I wish I could tell her. She'd understand how funny it is. She'd laugh.

CHAPTER TWENTY-SIX

In October 2000, Gretchen and I went to Austin, Minnesota, as the representatives of our father, Dreamy Dick Eberhart (as he had been known when a teenager, sometimes fondly and sometimes derisively), who, at ninety-six, was not a traveling man any longer.

We went to accept, in Dad's name, the honor of his high school rebuilding and renaming its library and media center after him. (Later, in 2001, Austin High named Dad a Distinguished Alumnus of the Century.)

Austin treated Gretchen and me most delightfully warmly. We were three-day-wonder media stars. It was the only time I have felt like a celebrity.

For several days, Gretchen and I did newspaper, radio, and TV interviews. We gave talks at four or five grade schools that had studied Dad's poems during the past several weeks. At the high school, we made a presentation that included showing a video of Dad reading a few poems and remembering old Austin. We ate Spamburgers and spent half a day canoeing on the Cedar

River, and we made it almost all the way to the falls (of course, without going over them).

We drove in the open, lead car during the Austin High School homecoming day parade. We were introduced during halftime at the homecoming football game, along with the homecoming king and queen (the Austin Packers won the game, of course). We attended a skit on the life of our father, written by schoolchildren and performed by them, and thus we had the pleasure of shaking hands with our grandfather A.L. and with our grandmother Lena, whom we had not had the pleasure to meet in real life—and we had the pleasure of chatting with our father, an eleven-year-old actor who appeared to have stepped right off a page of a Mark Twain novel.

Our days in Austin were very moving. One TV interview was filmed next to the library in a park—the park that once was Dad's front acreage at Burr Oaks. When the interview was over, I sat on a bench where Dad might have sat on a tree trunk, and I wondered what I should say during my big speech the next day at the official opening of the Richard Eberhart poetry library.

Why should students in the year 2000 care about this guy who was 1,500 miles and eighty years distant from them? And then it came to me why, and next day I told the assembled officials, townsfolk, and students why they should care.

"My father was an ordinary student, no scholar, but he tried *everything*. As a young man, he was a singer—who found his song. It doesn't matter what your song is," I told the audience. "What matters is this. It is your job, right now, to find your song. Right now. Right now in your lives; right now is the time for you to find it. And the reason why my father is important to you—to you who are the age he was when he was here in this very spot—the reason my father is important to you is that once, years ago, right here, he was one of you—*and he found his.*"

My speech was well received. This speech from the son of the poet, who loved his dad and believed deeply in the need we all have to find our "songs"—whatever is our tuneful and our deepest inspiration.

In Austin, at fourteen, Dad wrote his first poem. He persisted then. At ninety-six, he still wrote . . . when the occasion presented itself.

"Dad, people ask me if you still write poetry."

He grinned. "I don't go chasing after them anymore, but if one comes along, I'll write it down."

Me? I had not been able to finish my third novel; the song of that book had gone still. But at fifty-four, I was one half of a loving marriage, Channa and I were excited by our four compelling children, I was respected by my colleagues for carrying on a successful career, I was respected by my customers because I had never once pressured them or dissembled about my product, and I was beginning to wonder—with excitement, since what I was living now was my own life—if living one's own life with success might not be another variety of song too.

After the public ceremony was over, Gretchen and I were driven to Oak Dale.

*   *   *

Now Oak Dale is prairie and nothing more. We disembarked from our car. By this time, my knees were weak, and my heart raced. Somewhere, close by, was *the place.* Addressing the crowds in Austin was one thing, but this was *The Visionary Farms. The Visionary Farms* is the verse drama Dad wrote in the early 1950s about "The Fall of the House of Eberhart," as he once jokingly referred to A.L.'s business loss and Lena's death when describing them to me. Dad was joking, but—by now you know Dad—he wasn't joking.

I've mentioned before the portentous tone that Dad used when he told and retold the famous tale, making it seem a tragedy such as Hamlet might have soliloquized upon at Elsinore. And that afternoon, at that very moment, there we were, at Dad's Elsinore.

Old battlefields have an eerie quality about them, and the more one has studied and lived within the memory of the battle, the more eerie the quality is. As Dad's son, I had studied about him and his life with an intensity I had scarcely lavished on anything else except my marriage, my children, and my work. Oak Dale was central to what I knew about Dad—it was the Ur story. The story was the fulcrum on which all else balanced.

I was also an actor, susceptible to stage management. This was the place—this was the stage set—where, metaphorically, the bodies lay strewn. My knees were weak.

We sauntered across the open land. Still shaken by the feeling of walking in my father's past, I veered away. I wandered in whatever direction my feet took me. No sound came there but the sound of a now-and-then wind.

I chanced upon the swimming pool. It is a big, empty, concrete-lined rectangular hole in the prairie. Over the years, dirt has sifted into the deep end of the pool, enough to support thin trees that scarcely reach above the rim. In places, the concrete apron of the pool has broken down. Time levels all things. The slow teeth of the land have their chew.

I stood on the lip of the pool, eighty years after Dad's footprint. He was not present to make another cannonball leap.

Had he been—ah, the emotion that should have swollen the air!

Weeping, Dad might have knelt—should his knees have borne the strain—and stroked the earth with his fingers. Then he might well have struggled back to his feet and looked widely away. He might have murmured the final lines of "The Groundhog," the most famous death poem of his youth.

I stood there in the whirling summer,
My hand capped a withered heart,
And thought of China and of Greece,
Of Alexander in his tent;
Of Montaigne in his tower,
Of Saint Theresa in her wild lament.

But Dad was not there. So, dutiful son, raised well in the language of English verse, I felt it my responsibility to poem-make for him.

Yet I had no words.

All around me was empty prairie, with a scatter of weathered farm buildings in the distance. Nothing beside remained.

I had no words of my own, but I did have the words of Shelley, another Romantic and a member in good standing of Dad's emoting and visionary tribe—

Nothing beside remains. Round the decay
Of that colossal wreck, boundless and bare
The lone and level sands stretch far away.

My father was not there, but, in Shelley's lines about that ancient, mighty King Ozymandias, of whom nothing beside remains, Dad's muse-wet spirit was there, drenching his son's mind with wetness of my own.

So Dad and I stood there, in my imagination, on the rim of the swimming pool. I put my arms around Dad. Dad put his arms around me. His face was scratchy as it had been when I was young, and now my face was scratchy too.

There, at *The Visionary Farms*, I loved my father for being human and for being flawed. I loved him for being a poet and for being grand, and for loving the muse just as much as he loved his own son, who was also a lover of the muse—the muse who is one more manifestation of the ultimate Father of us all.

CHAPTER TWENTY-SEVEN

"Where are they?" asked Channa, frantic. "The sun sets at 7:13. What time is it?"

"It's 6:51."

"Oh! We'll never make it."

"We have twenty-two minutes. Maybe—if they come right now . . ."

"But think what's left to do!"

"We've done everything we *know* to do. We can't be responsible for what we don't know to do."

And we *had* done everything we knew to do.

We had done everything to *kasher* (make kosher) our kitchen and to set the rest of our house to rights for what was to be our third *Shabbaton*, which was to begin in twenty-two minutes. Our Orthodox rabbi was on his way to our house, with his wife and his five children, and we were to have a special Shabbat, away from the synagogue—a time of prayer and ceremony and learning and song.

We had needed to prepare. We had lit dim lights in the

bedrooms where lights were forbidden to be turned on or off during the next twenty-four hours; we had left strategic lights on in hallways so the rabbi and his family could find their way to the bathroom if they needed to do so after dark; we had laid out disposable plastic utensils and paper plates on the dining table, so we would not need to worry if a *dairy* knife should touch a *meat* plate; we had boiled lots of eggs and peeled them already so no peeling work would be required during the next twenty-four hours; we had laid out fruit and kosher peanut butter and crackers; we had cleaned and scrubbed as we usually do for a party, but with special care to place the *meat* cutlery, dishes, cutting board, cooking utensils, and sink scrubber on one side, while we placed the *dairy* cutlery, dishes, cutting board, cooking utensils, and sink scrubber on the other side. Some kosher kitchens have two refrigerators, so meat and dairy can be separated completely, but we had at least separated them inside our single refrigerator onto their separate shelves.

Channa asked, "Did you put the Bible on the table?"

"Yes, you already asked me. No carrying."

"No, Dikkon, you *can* carry something inside your house, just not outside. I just want the Bible to be available."

"Here," I said, "sit down. You're going to wear yourself out."

"I can't sit, Dikkon. I can't."

"Maybe they'll come in the next two minutes."

"You're sure you've thought of everything?"

"Yes. I think I have—*oh, no!* No, I haven't. I haven't taped the refrigerator light. If someone opens the door, the light will go on automatically."

I leaped up and dashed for the barn to get some duct tape to tape the trigger down inside the refrigerator door frame so it could not move and turn on the light when the door opened. And just at that moment the rabbi arrived in his big Suburban, having rushed all the way from Montreal, arriving with sixteen minutes to spare.

Frenzy.

All the suitcases needed to be inside and in the bedrooms within sixteen minutes—no carrying while outside on Shabbat.

"Dikkon, help me," the rabbi called urgently. He stopped herding the rebbetzin (the title for a rabbi's wife) and his children with the carrying. "I've got forty kosher chickens cut up in the back, on ice, but the ice will melt. Do you have anything—a second refrigerator maybe, or a freezer?"

What? Now? *Forty chickens?*

Twelve minutes!

"There's a freezer in the barn, but it's partly full."

"I'll back the car up to the barn. Hurry."

The rabbi's daughters and the rebbetzin were moving through the house efficiently, and when they saw some non-kosher arrangement, they worked with Channa to make it right.

Meanwhile, eight minutes to go.

The chicken boxes were large, flat, waxed cardboard with ice and chicken parts inside, no plastic bags or other storage. The boxes were already dripping melted water and chicken fat. Into the freezer the boxes went until the freezer was stuffed full. There were still more chickens.

I grabbed a large plastic trash can, splashed it a few times inside with the hose, slapped a trash bag into it, and the rabbi and I began packing it with handfuls of ice and dropping the remaining chicken parts onto the ice.

Four minutes.

"You finish; I must clean myself."

While I was annoyed at the rabbi for this sudden chicken calamity, it was funny, too, and I finished packing the ice and the meat. I wrapped two beach blankets around the trash bag and consigned it and its chickens to fate.

Suddenly, it was 7:13.

In the house, the rabbi began to chant. I closed the barn door from the outside and stood next to the Suburban for a moment. From inside the house, I could hear the chanting. My hands were chilled by the ice, and my sleeves and my shirt and my arms were smeared with chicken guts. Deliberately, I breathed slowly. This was Shabbat, after all, and I needed to be calm.

This was not how Channa and I were accustomed to throwing a party, and my desire to appear calm struggled against my annoyance at the rabbi. I realized the rabbi would chide me for this thought. He would say that we were *not* throwing a party. He would say that we were serving the Lord by observing His commandments for the hallowing of Shabbat. There was no *party* involved.

He would be correct. Clearly, Channa and I still had much to learn about Orthodox living. But it still *felt* that seven people arriving for the weekend was a party.

After our initial prayers, I voiced what was for me a major question. "But what if it was sunset, and you were still two miles away?"

"I would park on the road. I've done it before. We would walk the rest of the way."

"But you couldn't carry stuff."

"Maybe you have a friend who isn't Orthodox who would drive to our car and bring back the suitcases."

"And carry them inside?"

"And carry them inside." Then he grinned. "And upstairs, too."

I was astonished at the image in my head. I was astonished to imagine our rabbi striding forward along the main road in Phippsburg, as the light faded from the sky and the pickups rumbled by, as though he were some transplanted Abram following whither God wilt. I was astonished by the image of a ragged collection of the rebbetzin and of their smaller and smaller children, each child hurrying to keep up.

*   *   *

Twenty-four hours later, what had turned out to be a semi-pleasing time of prayer and learning came to its end. It was sundown on Saturday. We enjoyed the ceremony for the ending of Shabbat, a ceremony both of regret and of anticipation, during which we snuffed out the sacred candles and thereby ushered back in the profane.

We took the tape off the light trigger in the refrigerator. We lit up the stove to make hot water for tea. The rabbi fired up his Suburban so he could drive it back from the barn to the parking area. Our Sabbath day was over.

The next morning, Christians went to church on their Sabbath, and the rabbi desired to pray beside the sea. As we ate our breakfast, we heard the call-to-worship bell rung at the Baptist church just down our road and on its other side.

The rabbi gathered his regalia, and I drove him to the mouth of the Kennebec River. I thought this would be a good spot for his prayers, since there are interesting rock formations, a long, sandy beach stretching out into the ocean, and a granite fort

constructed to defend our shipbuilding center from British dep-
redations during the War of 1812. I drove the long way around
to the mouth of the river in order to show the rabbi more of our
countryside. Going the long way, we passed the Baptist church.

"It's a nice-looking church," I remarked to the rabbi, "isn't
it? So New England-y."

"Yes, it is," he replied.

The rabbi and I arrived at the mouth of the river. The tide
was low, so the rock formations at the base of the fort were at
their most exposed where they stretched out toward the sea.
In a straight line, Maine's coast between New Hampshire and
Canada is 226 miles long. However, if you were to walk our
actual shoreline, you would walk 3,478 miles. Anything might
have happened along those many crinkled promontories and
bays, but what happened near our fort during the next ninety
minutes was unusual, at least, if not unique.

Our rabbi was a short, powerful, eager man of intense awareness of the laws of his God. He radiated the same singularity of
being that I had admired before in Robert Frost and in Scott
Nearing—he did not seem; he was.

We two stood beside my car near the fort. It was a bright
morning with a firm breeze, and it was cool. Because it was
early Sunday, a number of "Burgers," as we call ourselves, were
walking the beach with their dogs or were already set up with
their lines in the water for stripers. The rabbi began to dress
himself for prayer. His ensemble was odd as compared with the
jeans, hoodies, and ball caps the rest of us wore. He wore a *kippa*
(skullcap) and *tallis* (prayer shawl), which were odd enough,
but when he began to wind on his phylacteries (shiny strips
of black leather that are bound numerous times around the

arm and neck and head, in part to fix a black box the size of a quarter-brick tightly onto the forehead), he became even odder.

He murmured rituals as he prepared himself. I remained silent. Then the rabbi strode to the end of the rock formations beside the fort, and striking a hierarchical pose, he began to chant. I sat down on the near end of the rocks, and I occupied space to make a barrier between my rabbi and the Burgers and their dogs, each curious about this new phenomenon. Just at that moment, I loved this man who was so willing not to seem.

While I protected my rabbi, I considered an important way that I differed from my dad. Unlike my father, I did not fool around with theology. Channa and I understood theology as vital. We were intense about this. There was nothing more important to us than the truth about God's nature and intention. There was nothing more important to us than how we might serve Him in the face of His revelation to us concerning His nature and His intention.

While I was fascinated by the Orthodox form of Judaism with which Channa and I were now engaged, even in Orthodox Judaism I had not found a way of belief which relieved the burden of my sin.

Though more than thirty-five years had passed, in my mind I still bore the image of that little girl who had died in the train wreck.

No, I had not killed the people on the train that my girl-friend and I should have ridden during our return. But I had omitted to help save them.

I still carried my guilt.

PART FOUR

"I need to tell you something, Dan."

"Okay."

"I need to tell you about the worst thing I ever did."

I took a deep breath and let it out. "When I was young,
I had a chance to avert an accident, and I didn't, and
people died."

"How old were you?"

"Twenty-one."

"And you've been carrying this weight now for how long?
Thirty-eight years?"

"Yes," I said and began to weep. "There was an eight-
year-old little girl."

"So she's in heaven."

"I don't know."

"What would you say if I told you that God has already forgiven you for what you did?"

I looked at him, eyes watering.

"Can God do that?"

"Of course. He already did."

I shook my head. "But why?"

"Because He wants to."

"Why? It makes no sense! Why should He want to?"

"Because He loves you."

"That's not what I was told."

"God forgave you because He wanted to, because He is responsible for what happens, not you."

I looked up.

"This is what evil does, Dikkon. Evil has kept you in prison for thirty-eight years. You've borne this weight for a long time, and it's not really there. It's gone."

And suddenly, it was.

When we were children, we loved to stand in a doorway and, with straight arms, to press as hard as we could against the two jambs with the backs of our hands, until our muscles screamed. Then, when we relaxed and stood away, our arms would float delightfully and effortlessly upward as though they were propelled by something other than ourselves. We did this again and again; it was so sweet.

In Pastor Dan's office, suddenly, my shoulders floated upward as though invited to ascend by God. No moment of weightlessness was ever sweeter for me, not even as a boy inside my father's open door.

Maybe that's what it feels like to be in heaven.

CHAPTER TWENTY-EIGHT

When Dad was ninety-three, Dartmouth honored him with a day of symposia, a late-afternoon reading by numerous poets, and a banquet afterward at the Hanover Inn, hosted by the college's president, James O. Freedman, and introduced by poet Cleopatra Mathis. Some of the poets honoring Dad were friends of many years: Allen Ginsberg, Donald Hall, Philip Booth, Dan Hoffman, Jay Parini, and Maxine Kumin. Dick Wilbur, Syd Lea, and others who could not attend sent testimonials, which were read aloud. By that time in my life, I had known these people for many years—I was an old hand who had gone in another career direction. Others among the attendees were newer in my acquaintance, such as Stephen Cory, Galway Kinnell, Christopher Keane, and William Logan.

Dad was the last to read. He was an old war horse hearing the trumpets blare; he read resoundingly and was funny.

After the reading, we invitees trooped across campus to the Inn. On this occasion, Allen Ginsberg was wearing shoes, so he was not refused his seat at the table. Of course, time had passed since the 1960s, and time changes what before was hot into what now is not.

Good speeches; good food. After dinner, a number of us stood, one after another, and read a favorite of Dad's poems to him while he sat beside the president and glowed. After a few of the poets had done their bit, I stood and read "Seals, Terns, Time."

The seals at play off Western Isle
In the loose flowing of the summer tide
And burden of our strange estate—

Resting on the oar and lolling on the sea,
I saw their curious images,
Hypnotic, sympathetic eyes

As the deep elapses of the soul.
O ancient blood, O blurred kind forms
That rise and peer from elemental water:

I loll upon the oar, I think upon the day,
Drawn by strong, by the animal soft bonds
Back to a dim pre-history;

While off the point of Jagged Light
In hundreds, gracefully, the fork-tailed terns
Draw swift esprits across the sky.

Their aspirations dip in mine,
The quick order of their changing spirit,
More freedom than the eye can see.

Resting lightly on the oarlocks,
Pondering and balanced upon the sea,
A gauze and spindrift of the world,

I am in compulsion hid and thwarted,
Pulled back in the mammal water,
Enticed to the release of the sky.

When I finished and sat down, Allen—who had perhaps been a little bored with the proceedings and had spent most of the after-dinner time amusing my daughters by drawing for them his little inventive animal-creature cartoons—said this: "Dikkon, that was you?"

I nodded.

"I had my eyes closed. I thought it was Dick reading; your diction is so exactly how he reads that poem—the rhythms, the emphases."

I smiled down the table at Allen and then at Dad. "Thank you" is what I said.

Had I still been an actor, Allen's remark would have been a fine compliment.

But I was not an actor. My intention had been to express my love for my father by assuring him that I had listened at his knee. My reading had not been mimicry; it had been gifting.

When the party was over, and we were clustering around, I was clustering mostly with Allen and thanking him for amusing my daughters.

Allen enlarged his point. "I've heard you do 'The Groundhog,' Dikkon. Sometimes you do it better than Dick does. He has mixed feelings about it, or used to anyway. Your mother told me once that Dick would refuse to read it in public at all—this would have been in the 1940s—jealous as he was of it for his other verse."

"Well," I laughed, "he did it twice this afternoon."

That was true. "The Groundhog" was the final poem Dad read. When he had finished it, and the audience was still absorbed in silence, Dad twinkled at them and said, "That was a good one. I'm going to do that one again."

And he did.

There was an Eberhartian death-in-life poignancy hovering over Allen's and my conversation, but which I did not know about at the time. Fewer than ten days later, on the day of my father's ninety-fourth birthday, Allen Ginsberg suffered his untimely demise.

R.I.P.

*   *   *

Time continued its work.

Dad was immortal, just as Grandmother and Scott Nearing had seemed to be. When Dad was about ninety-six, his geron-tologist told me that there was nothing left that could kill him. "Oh, he'll die," he assured me. "But he's survived everything that kills people. He won't die *of* something. One day, he'll just stop."

Dad was aware of one benefit of his advanced age. Once, when he was in his midnineties, he asked me, "You know the critics?"

"Yes."

"They're all dead."

"Yes?"

"And I'm not."

When Dad became a centenarian, Gretchen and I threw a big party at his retirement home, and people from all his walks of life attended; he was the retirement home's oldest resident.

One of the guests at the party asked me what I thought Scott Nearing and my father had in common. Without hesitation, I replied, "Joy."

No one who knew Scott Nearing well during his later years would describe him as a joyful man, at least not in the conventional sense of the word. In fact, he was utterly bleak in his assessment of the failure of humankind. His diagnosis was so bleak that, if it were put in religious terms—which he would not have done himself—it was gnostic. All created things are evil, including humankind, and there is neither grace nor salvation. Only a very few—the knowing ones—may attain wisdom, but through their own effort alone.

Nevertheless, as I answered the question, my intuition was that Scott was joyful in a personal sense.

Both Dad and Scott lived lives without much second-guessing. Oh, I know my father had worries, and I am sure Scott did as well. One cannot be human and have it otherwise. But the essential quality that binds them together in my mind is their deep commitment to their muses. That commitment brought them joy—the joy of doing what they knew they were meant to do.

My grandmother was joyful as well. She was joyful in the burgeoning of her family, in its success, and in her ever-widening circle of acquaintance. While the two men played to the audience of their own imaginations and were at base concerned with their impact on history, Grandmother played to the audience of *our* imaginations—we of her extended family—and was content to make herself, for us, a legend of graciousness, of welcome, of taste, of daring, and of apparent immortality.

Another year went by. Dad pushed life's boulder uphill during another twelve months.

It became more awkward for our children to visit Dad in his retirement home because his bedroom seemed ever smaller— there were six of us, and the children were grown now; where does one stand?

Among all the children, the one who was least discomfited by their grandfather in his decrepitude was Sam. Sam would sit beside Dad on the bed, and he would pat Dad on the chest, and he would say, "You are a good man. You are a good man." Then he would lay his head on Dad's chest.

The blazing lyricist and the Down syndrome word-stumbler— at one.

Dad's 101st birthday party was much more modest than had been his 100th. As Gretchen and I joked together, we were saving the next big one for the 110th.

As the 101st birthday party wound down, Dreamy Dick reclined on his bed with a cup of chocolate milk—upon which he mostly subsisted in those days. He had been unusually energetic during the past four or five hours, very reluctant that the party should end.

Mom had been very present to him. He kept insisting that my family and I not drive back to Maine that evening: "Your mother and I so much want you to stay."

At one point Dad got up to go and see if Mom might be awake from her nap because he was certain she would want to see more of us. I took him aside and told him that Mom was dead. He was saddened to hear of it, but as he sat down again on the bed, I had the sense that he didn't perceive her location as being so very far distant anymore. Not so very far away as the Land of the Dead had used to be.

We stayed a little longer. Gretchen and her husband, Michael, had already left, and Dad was tired now. It was time to go. But Dad kept rousing whenever we made to leave, so we would settle back down.

Then I had an idea.

I read to Dad—and to my family—of the exploits of Eberhart the Noble. I've mentioned this man before. He is one of our most remote and most puissant ancestors. He was born March 13, 1265, in what was then Swabia (more recently Bavaria). He was kin to the Holy Roman Emperor. At the age of fifteen, single-handedly, Eberhart the Noble created the Duchy of Wurttemberg. When he died sixty-one years later—June 5, 1325—he had spent forty-six years as duke, and most of that time he was fighting either offensive or defensive war. Other dukes in the area had laughed at him when, as a boy, he had bought his seal and set up his throne and commenced to do business as ruler. But forty-six years later, he was no laughingstock. He had annexed all their lands.

That's *seven hundred years* of directly traceable Eberhartian lineage. Rome herself scarcely lasted longer.

Seven of my centenarian fathers, standing in a row, could shake the Duke's hand.

Eberhart the Noble and his wife, Irmingard, had three sons, all of whom were named Ulrich. The middle of these men succeeded his father on the throne. I've mentioned him before: Eberhart of the Rushing Beard, which name he earned by reason of his impulsiveness, which was remarkable, and by reason of his long beard, which flew out behind him as he dashed.

This second Duke carried on the reign that his father had begun, and thus was initiated the 443-year supremacy of the Eberharts in Wurttemberg. When you read about our ancestors, you find that, as a line, we are said mostly to have been strong, resolute, kindly rulers, much beloved by our people. Consistently, the four centuries of Eberhart dukes are characterized as being deeply religious (Lutheran, once that division began), militarily savvy, great riders and hunters, valuers of learning, and notable writers and poets.

Ah—poets!

Of course, we had our faults and made our mistakes. In fact, the end of the *Regnum Eberhartium* (Dad would love that usage!) in 1723 was occasioned by one such mistake. An act of polygamy by Duke Leopold Eberhart was the culprit.

Duke Leopold was another of the Eberharts whose learning was broad. He explored religious writing of his time, and he found himself interested in the Koran. Under its aegis, he married three wives. This outraged his people, and it weakened the claim of any of his heirs to the throne, as all of them were illegitimate. Duke Leopold attempted to rescue the situation, first by appealing for a favorable verdict to the Pope, but to no avail, and then to the King of France, who wouldn't assist either, and then by selling the dukedom to his cousin Eberhart Ludwig.

However, in the confusion, an even more distant cousin of the Eberharts—and a Catholic to boot—one Charles Augen, was able to snatch the throne. All of what is now Germany at that time was convulsed with civil and religious fervor—the

Catholic–Protestant Thirty Years' War had weakened internal cohesion. The Catholics were in the ascendancy. When Charles VI died in 1740 without clearly delineated issue, the entire structure based on the Hapsburg line began to crumble.

And the Eberharts, as we have seen before, brought their religious fervor, their work ethic, their high-mindedness, and their literary accomplishment to America.

I sat beside the bed of my father, the 101-year-old poet, and I read to him about the exploits of the Eberharts—formerly sung by the German poets Schiller and Kerner—until he fell asleep.

*   *   *

On June 7, I was on a sales trip in the mountains of way-northern Maine. It was a grand day of high clouds, great stabbing shafts of sunlight, and springing green. The mountains looked like a German Romantic painting. Suddenly, at noon, it came into my mind that if this were the day when Dad died, it would be a very good day for that.

When I drove down out of the mountains, my cell phone buzzed. A message awaited me. The message from Gretchen was "Dad fell at noon. Stand by. This may be *IT*."

By June 8, we knew indeed that this was *IT*, and that my father's call to me the day before—the call of his spirit—across six hundred miles of New England, had not been a trial run.

I spurred my car south and west at a furious roar. As I passed through Portsmouth, New Hampshire, the sky darkened until it was the blackest I believe I have ever seen in my life. A thunderstorm of cataclysmic proportions was brewing.

The thunderstorm hit ten miles later. It hit so hard that our line of cars could scarcely crawl. Vision forward was hardly possible. Lightning slashed. Thunder shook the very surface of the road. Entire trees were whipped like straws. Limbs broke off, and I bulled past them, snapping their branches under my tires, not knowing how much time I had left.

I had been following the car ahead, perhaps twenty feet from its bumper, the only thing I could see. Presently, its driver gave up and pulled aside. There was another car ahead, a green car. I tried to close with it. I crept closer and closer. Then I saw its license plate. The license plate bore a single word: *POETIK*.

I followed *POETIK* through the storm and arrived at my father's deathbed in time.

Poet Richard Eberhart died June 9, 2005, two months after his 101st birthday. He died of complications following a fall and of the muse finally calling him home.

*   *   *

The death of a man who is 101 cannot be termed a surprise, but it can be—and it was—a shock.

I adored my father. As I grew, I longed both for his attention and for his affirmation, as most lads do. I received both.

Sometimes, when I wished he would toss a football with me, as other fathers did with their sons, he might instead have written a poem that should last one hundred years. I didn't get the football that day, and I was disappointed. But in my life I was tossed other sorts of balls, elegiac spheres that danced on my fingertips. I was privileged to observe my father playing verbal catch—and creating incandescent beauty—with the gods of song and idea.

Later, when I was a man, I received attention and affirmation from other sources than my father. When I was in despair at my badness, I wished it were he who could save me. He could not. It was not Dad's job to save me.

Still later, when I was an older man, and when I had begun to father my father—for example, when Gretchen and I decided to sell his house in Hanover and needed to bandage his pain at the loss—it was a wrench to find that we were now the ones to offer comfort.

There were times when I felt annoyed with Dad's self-involvement or dreaminess or obtuseness.

Yet my father loved his two children, utterly. He loved us as *he* was given to love. He could not possibly have given more, for we humans are finite beings powerless to be more than we are.

At the time Dad died, I was a Jew. Not a very pious Jew, it is true, but a Jew nonetheless.

I was a Jew.

I was fatherless.

And I was lost.

CHAPTER TWENTY-NINE

I was lost.

But perhaps I might be found.

I had heard about foundness.

There were souls who had been found.

Somewhere there had to be a compass to point me the way.

One day, at the end of the day, more than a year after Dad died, I came in from my car and dropped my computer bag by the wall where we hang our outer coats. Channa was still in the office in the barn. I was tired and grumpy.

I went into the living room and sat on the couch. I felt particularly vulnerable, but at the same time willing to expose myself. I didn't say anything or do anything; I just sat.

In time, Channa came in from the office.

Usually I put introspection aside when Channa comes off work, and I ask her about her present project and how it's going. But this time I said to her, "I can't do it myself."

"What?"

"I mean it. This is hard for me to say. But I can't do it myself."

Channa sat down next to me on the couch. "Do what?"

"Everything. Life. All of it." I was still for a moment and then said, "I thought I could, but I can't."

"Oh, I get it." She smiled. "It's the end of the month, isn't it? And there'll never be another sale."

I laughed. "No. It's not that. The month was fine. No. It's not that. It's—everything else."

Channa watched me for a moment. I was looking at the painting over the fireplace but was aware of her eyes on my profile. Then, "Hold that thought," she said. "I'll put on the soup. Then I want to know more."

I sat still. There were a few minutes of kitchen sounds and then Channa went to the bottom of the stairs and called up to Sam to set the table. When she returned, she asked, "You want anything?"

I shook my head. She sat sideways on the couch with her legs pulled up under her. "Tell me."

"I'm good at a lot of things, I know that. But I'm fifty-nine years old, and I'm tired of carrying everything inside myself. I don't think I can do it anymore. It's like the emperor's new clothes. Someday, everyone's going to see that there's nothing here. It's just—I don't know, ego. And burden. And pride, I suppose. Pride that I can do it my way—but I can't."

She touched me to reassure me that she was there, but she didn't say anything, wanting me to go on.

I took a deep breath and let it out. "I need help."

I turned to look at her for the first time. "I need help."

To me, as a husband, it seemed I had just made a dizzying revelation, but my wife did not appear to be shaken by it. Of course, in my heart, I knew my revelation was neither dizzying nor likely to shake Channa. But it felt dizzying.

"I need help," I repeated. "I can't do it alone."

"You're not alone."

"I know I'm not alone."

Channa took my hand, the one closest to her. I looked away again and took my hand away and ran both hands through my hair.

"I don't like to admit that I can't do it all."

"Yes."

"But I can't."

There was a long silence. Then Channa said, "No one can, Dikkon."

"No. I guess not. But I don't know where all this is going. It frightens me that I don't know where it's going."

"That's part of the asking for help. If you knew where it was all going, you wouldn't be asking for help. And all of us, we all of us need to ask for help."

"Who said that?" I wanted to know.

"I don't know. Probably everyone. But I said it now."

We were quiet. Sam came downstairs, gave me a hug, we exchanged a few words about how his work at the college dining hall had gone that day, and then he went to set the table. He's short, muscular, handsome, athletic—and funny. Quite a guy.

"I just feel I need help," I repeated.

"We need help. It breaks my heart when I know there's something you're thinking, and you can't find a way to tell me. It makes me imagine all kinds of awful things. You need to not be afraid of whatever you're thinking. We can handle it. But you need to tell me what you're thinking."

I sighed. "What I'm thinking is, I can't do it myself."

CHAPTER THIRTY

I woke up.

It was Sunday. It was March. It was windy and cold on the coast of Maine.

I had no idea how to solve my problem.

"I guess I'll try the church across the road this time," I said to Channa. I sighed. "There's got to be an answer. Somewhere there's got to be an answer."

Channa was still in bed. She was propped against pillows with a coffee cup and a book. She pulled the blankets higher. Her glance was affectionate but without anticipation.

"You go. I'm too shy."

"Shall I need a tie, do you suppose?"

"This is Maine."

I swung out of bed. The floor was cold. I hurried to dress—collared shirt but no tie. From up the road, the church bell rang.

"Tell me all about it," Channa said.

"Back soon." I bent and kissed her. "How long can one more church service take, after all?"

I went downstairs. I didn't see the children. Someone had eaten cereal and not cleaned up afterward.

I was too tense to eat.

I pulled on a winter coat and stepped out the door.

Watch out!

Here comes the Jew.

* * *

I walked across the road. I just—walked across the road.

I walked through the church's door. A person handed me a bulletin. I sat in the rearmost pew. Shortly, the pastor asked us to stand and to sing a hymn. So far, so good.

But then it got bad.

Oh no. They're not going to do that, are they?

There I stood, a Jew, in the back pew of Small Point Baptist Church, Phippsburg, Maine. I was surrounded by strangers. We of the assemblage had just finished two hymns, and instead of asking us to sit down and to listen to his sermon, Pastor Dan had just instructed us to turn around and to greet one another: "If you see someone you don't know, greet that person."

Oh, darn.

I remembered that this embarrassment of handshaking began when I was young. It was all the rage among Episcopalians. It was going to change our lives. We called it "passing the peace." What I had wanted instead when I was young was to sit in decent isolation and not to foist an unwanted salutation on our neighbors in the opposite pew.

Really, as I thought of it here, at this church, it was too bad that they should stoop to phony theatrics. Until this moment, this church had seemed such a nice little church, with its white steeple outside, and its numbered pews, and its plain-Jane decor inside. Too, I liked its rugged, old wooden cross, which was hanging in its apse, free of any corpus or folderol.

Oh well, I thought to myself, *it'll be over in two minutes.*

Dutifully, I stepped from my pew and held out my hand to the man in the pew before me. He took my hand in two of his, looked me deeply in the eye, and said, "How nice it is to have you here."

I was confused. He didn't know me.

The woman next to him took my hand. "We're so very glad to have you with us today." Maybe I was wrong; maybe I did know these people from somewhere after all. Ours is a tiny town, placed at the end of a long peninsula out into the ocean. Might I have seen these people at the school, perhaps? Maybe the store?

We were thirty seconds into the greeting period. Another man took my hand. "It's a real pleasure to see you here this morning. How are you?"

"Um, fine."

Around me, people had debouched from their pews and jammed the aisles, hugging one another, shaking hands, kissing, laughing.

What was going on? This was like nothing I had experienced before in a church, or in a synagogue for that matter. It went on and on. By the time the pastor waved us back to attention, seven or eight minutes had passed, and I was ten pews away from my seat. I'd been greeted—truly hailed—by twenty people, each equally delighted to have me—me!—here at church with them. Also, somehow, by that time, I was greeting them back as though I knew them!

This was cordiality of a quality I had never experienced before in a holy setting. It was beyond mere amiability. Something else was active here, something else was—well—something else was walking in those aisles.

I sat back down. I recalled my seminarian past and remembered Jesus and that unnamed disciple, whom Jesus loved the best. I'd always been interested in that fellow, whom the evangelist John fails to name: Who was that man? Most scholars assume that he was John himself, but suddenly I had a new idea of who else he might be. Though a stranger, I had just been sincerely welcomed by this Christian community. Maybe that disciple, the one who is unnamed, can't be named. Maybe that disciple can't be named because no one knows him yet. Maybe that unknown disciple, whom Jesus loves the best, is always just the newest one to come.

We were a mere fifteen minutes into the service, and—the newest one to come—I felt a hook sink in, which is a metaphor appropriate to our fisherman community. Peter was trolling for me, and I was caught.

But I am a Jew!

I admonished myself: *Dikkon, you are a Jew. This Christianity stuff is not meant for you. This whole Christianity stuff is—well, I don't know what it is, but it isn't for you.*

But then why am I here?

There was that hook in my mouth. I could feel it.

So what was I to do? Could I shake myself free of the hook?

After only fifteen minutes at this church I could see myself shaking up our family's entire existence. Everything would need to change.

Dikkon, I said to myself, *what's wrong with you? Get a grip!*

But Channa—I pointed this out to myself—Channa was deeply interested to volunteer as a counselor with a pregnancy help center, Care Net. While going through the training, which included a practical introduction to Christian theology regarding how a counseling volunteer might interact with a frightened young woman, Jewish Channa asked the director how someone who is not Christian could possibly do this job. Channa wanted to help these clients. How could she do so if she didn't have the faith that the director believed was essential? The director responded that it was a good question and she was praying about it. At the time, Channa took this response to mean, "I'm thinking very seriously about it." But—really—it meant much more than that.

For me, of course, intellectual diffidence had always been the comfortable cloak that protected me from the impact of any big new concept that might come swaggering up and force me to alter my ideas. All my intellectual arrangements were precisely set in their careful places, like object d'arte on my mantel piece, to be regarded with satisfaction.

I have a PhD after all!

Yes, I had begun this March morning by crossing our road to this church, but I was not consciously aware of any hankering I might have for some swaggering new idea with its ruffian insistence that I pay attention!

A woman—not Channa—once challenged me thus: "You're so cerebral, Dikkon. The highest compliment you can pay anything is that it's interesting! Interesting, ha! Why don't you ever *do* something instead?"

Hooked, now I wanted to do something, but I didn't know how. I didn't even know how to wonder about how.

Next in the service came prayer requests. The pastor knew of some, and others were raised from the floor. I listened to them all: this person had decided finally to have the operation, and it was scheduled for next week; that person was traveling to see grandchildren; another was struggling because the pains had returned; a ten-year-old requested prayers for her teacher who had a cold; one man tearfully thanked the congregation for its prayers for his son, an army rifleman deployed in Iraq, whom the father reported to be in greater spirit now than he had been before, when the father had first solicited prayers.

For ten minutes, we discussed the medical and emotional urgencies of the congregation. This, too, was new to me. Who were these people—what was this congregation—that it should so commonly share these intimate details?

The world Channa and I knew shared such details neither so publicly nor so effortlessly. The world we knew—partially Jewish, partially secular—that world validated Thoreau's statement that "the mass of men lead lives of quiet desperation."

I myself lived a life of quiet desperation. And yet, in this church this morning, I sensed that these people around me, somehow or other, these people around me were free from quiet desperation.

From their prayer requests, I knew they had troubles, plenty of them. They spoke about their troubles out loud in this place—odd enough. But by doing so, they invited their community to support them in their troubles. I watched the faces of the others who were listening to the prayer requests. Suddenly, I had a new thought.

Regarding those others who were listening, they did not appear to be unnerved by the troubles of the others, or embarrassed to hear of them. Perhaps—it suddenly occurred to me—those others instead were grateful to be trusted to help, to be given the opportunity to help.

About that, theologically, here's what stunned me. That whole dynamic of support within a community would make sense only if it were under the aegis of a God who *personally* knew these individuals and who *personally* cared. Otherwise the whole dynamic could not work.

Now the pastor gathered us into prayer. Responding to the requests, the pastor was plainspoken in his prayer. Completing my theological astonishment, he prayed as though he were speaking, seriously but familiarly, with a trusted, knowledgeable, and wise counselor before whom all the details might usefully be laid.

But how could God—actual God—know us personally? It did not compute.

We were twenty-five minutes into the service, maybe thirty. After the prayers, we made an offering, and we sang one more hymn. The church had a good choir of local singers with a few particularly graced voices; it was led by a woman who was evidently the pastor's wife and who played the piano. I was grateful to see one face in the choir I knew, a lobsterman friend. Then, finally, we settled down to hear the pastor's sermon, which—I learned later—is called a "message" at this church, a much more downscale and modest term than what I had been accustomed to using as a youngster.

At that time, as a Jew, I believed Jesus was a wise man, a stimulating teacher, etc., etc., but that he wasn't, you know, a manly man. In my understanding of him at that time there was something too elusive, too ethereal: he wasn't like the rest of us men are. The rest of us men—if you're a man, you'll know this, and if you're a woman, you will too—we men run on die-hard batteries of sex and competition. Whatever smooth ways we have learned in our lives, those are just ways that advantageously channel our power and keep us out of social trouble. Whoever Jesus may have been to those who "got it" about him, he was fey to me.

Yet here was this pastor, preaching from 1 Peter. Later, he told me it must have been part of God's plan, but that very Sunday morning he broke off from his prepared remarks and made an analogy that turned upon army discipline. In the course of his discursion, I learned he had come to the pastorate after a fourteen-year career as a master sergeant and jumpmaster in the Eighty-Second Airborne Division. Here was a man who had trained to the peak of perfection in leading and protecting men who jump out of airplanes into combat, and he spoke of being called by Jesus instead to preach.

You may be sure his résumé caught my attention.

Pastor Dan delivered a thirty-minute message that was intelligent, direct, biblical, and plain. He was not hortatory; he was inviting. All together, his message was a compellingly attractive occurrence, and others of them have been so since; he is a winsome master of homiletics.

One thing that both thrilled and mystified me: in that message, Pastor Dan made reference to several verses from the Hebrew Bible, known to his congregation as the Old Testament. He incorporated the experience of the Jews into his New Testament message as naturally as one incorporates salt into eggs. I felt disoriented. Here was a Baptist preacher who took Torah seriously and who placed it, with accurate nuance, in its proper context!

What was I to *do*?

There came one final hymn, and then the service ended with what I have learned is the pastor's signature exhortation, "Have a great week in the Lord!"

Ninety minutes into my acquaintance with this pastor, I felt compelled to confess to him. Not that I expected absolution; I didn't know much about Baptists, but I knew I shouldn't expect that.

During the pastor's introduction, before the service began, he had invited any visitors to fill out a card. This I never do. However, after the service, I got one of the cards and filled it out. Then, instead of slinking out the door—this I always do—I approached him, handed him my visitor card, and introduced myself. Awkwardly, I blurted something about being Jewish, and living right across the road, and wanting—maybe—some time to speak with him, and would that be all right?—all in one sentence. "That would be fine," he responded. We had a vigorous conversation of ten minutes—oddly, it felt as though he already knew me—and then I hastened myself home in a hurry.

A half hour later, I concluded my excited report to Channa by saying, "I'm going to call him sometime," meaning later. Knowing her diffident husband and aware, therefore, of what I meant, Channa said, "No, call now."

Pastor Dan answered my first ring, and without preamble, he said, "Hi, Dikkon. I was sure you would call this afternoon." How had he been sure? How had he pronounced my name correctly?

We made a date for a visit to our home. I assumed it would be a visit of half an hour for a cup of tea and a cookie. I assumed it would have a cool, New England austerity about it. Not so.

Three hours after Pastor Dan sat down on our couch, he had elicited the details of both Channa's and my spiritual journeys. Also, he had offered a first answer to my plaint, "But still I don't get it about Jesus."

"Jesus," he said, "is the love in the fellowship."

"Oh!"

I said no more, but I made what was the beginning of a connection. *That's* who had been passing among the pews.

Goodness.

What a predicament.

CHAPTER THIRTY-ONE

During the next several months, Channa and I became regular attendees at South Point Baptist Church. The posture we took with ourselves was that we were attending church across the road merely because we liked being there and the people were welcoming and the preacher was dynamic and the commute was short and the messages were a mixture of Torah and the New Testament. And, after all, we didn't need to *be* Christians to go there.

We also began to develop friendships with Christians—of course, just because they were there. While our new friends had their individual personalities and problems, of course, as a general characteristic they seemed to brood less and to keep their chins up more than we were accustomed to experience among the denizens of our skeptical, sophisticated, worldly, Jewish circle.

As I had experienced at church that first Sunday, our new friends were entirely open about their problems. I was shut about our problems. My understanding was that our problems were not to be spoken of until we had solved them . . . and not then, either, because we had solved them. Channa is a much more natural sharer than I am, but even she was accustomed to employ a decorous reserve when discussing our troubles.

I particularly remember an electrician who wired our barn office: he cast off downheartedness when he was blue. He just—cast it off. When questioned about this odd nonchalance, he reported to me that he gave his troubles over to the Lord. "God's in charge," he averred, "not me."

How charmingly innocent, I remember thinking.

And then I remember thinking: *But what if he's right?*

* * *

One day I woke with an idea. It had formed itself during a dream, the sort of dream one retains after awakening. I was excited because this idea seemed to be a breakthrough. I didn't speak of it to Channa right then; I needed time to let my idea rise, like bread when left alone in a warm spot. It was Sunday. The church would be just such a comfortable nook.

After church, Channa prepared dinner and then nestled into a corner of the couch with her Charles Colson book and a glass of wine. She wore a fitted red cotton blouse with a scoop neck, decorated with gold threading around its neck and wrists, and she wore clinging black velour pants—as always, both colorful and simple at the same time. Her earrings were dangling gold and onyx ones I had bought her for a recent birthday—pretty against her neck.

I came in from mulching the gardens for winter and sat down in the rocking chair, rather winded. "I've thought of something."

Channa put down her book and looked at me over her glasses. "Yes?"

"This has to do with Jesus. I think I'm getting it."

Channa removed her glasses and bedded them among the black curls on the top of her head. "Tell me."

The house smelled good from cooking. It was autumn, the leaves were at their peak of gorgeousness before dropping for the winter, the day was windy and bright. None of the children were at home just then, so it was comfortable to discuss these things in the living room, things that were always on our minds but especially so after church.

I was quiet for a moment. Outside, a brisk, dry wind stirred the trees. Soon enough, the year would hunker down, draw in on itself, prepare to be still; it was time for us to focus.

"Here's what I think," I said. "Jesus is like the *translation*, that's what I'm thinking." I spoke slowly. I wanted to present my idea clearly, so Channa would understand. "I was thinking this when I woke up. I never *got it* about Jesus before. God, sure, I could get it about God. That's one of the things I liked about Judaism. You didn't need a translation. You could wrestle with God in the desert, cheek to cheek, sweat to sweat. Or talk with Him outside your tent, like Abraham. It's very manly, Judaism, that way. You don't need Jesus in between you." I laughed.

I sat in the rocking chair but did not rock. "What I'm thinking now is that it turns out God is just too ungraspable for us mere humans. We all of us yearn to touch God, to grab hold of Him for dear life."

I looked at Channa, who nodded. "You know how a youngster shakes and pummels his father?" I smiled, remembering wrestling with James in our Connecticut house. "Like when your son is angry or scared, and he needs to know you're stronger than he is, no matter how hard he struggles in your arms?"

"Yes."

"We're like the youngsters. But we can't get our arms around God's neck. It's too far to reach. God's too—other. We'll get burned if we actually touch God. So what we need is exactly what God gave to us. He gave us Himself in a way that we *can* grasp Him and struggle with Him. He gave us Himself, but *as one of us*. He made Himself man but was actually God at the same time. That is, God became Jesus.

"So Jesus is the *translation*. He's God we *can* grapple with. And when we do, we are held so tight by Him that we know— we absolutely know—there's something stronger and bigger and more powerful than we are, no matter how angry or frightened we are, and that the stronger and bigger Thing loves us enough to wrestle with us, and to test us, and that we are therefore safe."

Channa thought about this, sipped from her glass, and then she said, "That's very good. But the way you describe it is a man thing. I like it, and I think you're right—for you. We women don't fight so much, I don't think. We want to protect and be protected."

"There's nothing about Jesus that isn't protective. That's one of the foundations." I stood up. "I'll have wine too." I returned from the kitchen with the liquid, deeply red, in my glass. Rich, fragrant: maybe this was what they drank at the Last Supper.

"And here's the other side of it. Much as we want to wrestle with God, and we have Jesus instead to wrestle with, we also hate that we need His protection. We want to do everything all on our own. So we hate Jesus as much as we love Him, and we kill Him. But we can't get rid of Him—the guy just won't stay dead. And that fact proves He *was* God after all, in the first place. Then there's nothing left for us to do but to worship Him."

I looked at Channa. She was taking it in. I like it when she takes it in.

"I used to think I understood God. All you need to do, I used to think, is you just listen to what the prophets say, and you read about them in the Bible, and you interpret history as being God's message. And the sum of those things is God. That's what I used to think.

"But what's happening to me now is that God is getting *harder* to understand for me, not easier. And as He gets harder, Jesus is stepping forward for me. Because He is more necessary now than ever, as the translation."

Channa smiled the smile that lights her face. "I know what you're saying." Then she settled her glasses back on her nose and picked up her book. "For you, I think it's becoming real. It's not real for me."

"Do you want it to be?"

"I'm just reading here, Dikkon. I'm just having a good time."

She paused, took another sip of wine, and tilted her head just so.

"But everything I read makes so much sense!"

CHAPTER THIRTY-TWO

"But Dad, how can you believe in a religion that condemns me to hell?"

Lena and I were on the beach, way down where the river meanders in. It was late fall. A cold wind blew off the ocean and stiffened our faces. For an hour we had discussed the gestation of her mother's and my magnetic attraction to Christianity, while we strode vigorously along. Now she stopped, turned to me, and grabbed my attention. Hers, now, was the question that stung.

"But how can you?"

"This is the hardest part for me, Lena, the eternal life part: how some people are saved by their acceptance of God's grace and others are lost because of their knowing rejection of it. I don't understand it myself."

Eyes glittering with anger: "You're ducking the question."

"Yes, I am. But I'm also telling the truth. I'm new to this. I don't understand all of it. I'm taking it on piece by piece."

"Not good enough, Dad."

"Listen. This is a process of understanding, and I'm at its beginning."

"So—" her feet planted—"while you're still figuring it out, I go to hell."

"Pastor Dan's point is that either the Bible is all true, or it's nothing. You read the end of the Bible—Revelation—and it tells what's going to happen at the end of time, and throughout the New Testament there's a clear awareness of the distinction between heaven and hell, and there's a growing sense in your mother and me that life is either about the truth or it's about a lie, and . . ."

"Yes?"

"Well . . ." I took a deep breath. "And that those who live in the lie are bound for hell." I shrugged. "Or so the Bible says."

"That's me, Dad."

"Lena, I don't know! It anguishes me not to know."

She snorted. "That's a comfort."

She turned into the wind, pushed her swirling brown hair away from her face, and pulled her parka more tightly closed at her neck. She's an intense woman with an open, oval, pretty face; snapping eyes; and a quick, sharp mind—our first child, a jewel.

"Lena, be patient. I'm trying to understand something that has been there always, or for thousands of years."

I stared at her, and she stared back.

I continued, "I'm thinking that maybe Christ really existed. If he did, then I can't just say, 'Oh, well, what's for dinner?' I have to say, 'What does that mean?'"

"It means I go to hell."

We walked in silence for a while. Eventually, Lena said, "This really troubles me."

"I know it does. I'm sorry. It does me, too."

She let out a heavy breath, took my arm, and for a moment, leaned her head against my shoulder, but that was awkward, walking.

"I love you," I said.

She gave me a soft punch on the shoulder.

I said, "Maybe there's a different way to think about all this."

"Maybe not."

"I've got a lot more to learn."

"Well then, Dad," she said, tabling the discussion with exasperation, "tell me all about it when you know."

But when we reached the car, I said, "Hell is death, absence from God, that's all. Heaven is eternal life, being present with God. If you're a believer, you'd prefer the latter. And if you're a believer, you'd prefer the latter for anyone you love, too. But if the person's life has been absent from God all along, then death absent from God—"

"I'm not absent from God."

"I know, Lena. I know. But my point is that death absent from God—even if it is eternal—can't be all that different from what's been experienced all along anyway."

"That's sophistry. You're still condemning me to hell."

"I'm not."

"Your religion is, Dad. And I resent it, big time."

*　　*　　*

Lena wasn't the only child to struggle with Channa's and my newfound attraction to Christianity. James also had issues with it. In keeping with his personality, James expressed his concerns on a more philosophical plane. He and I had debates on many topics but especially on the question of predestination (the idea that God controls everything that happens to us) versus free will (the idea that we have a choice).

That's a very difficult conundrum for any intellectual thinker, at that time myself included.

James would ask, "But how does it work?"

I would answer using words from books or from Pastor Dan, which were not yet words from my own heart.

Then I might say, "There are lots of things about God that we can't understand. That's because He's God and we're not. It's not our place to understand them. So that's where faith comes in."

"How can you have faith in something you don't understand?"

"I have faith in the fact that your mother and I love each other, but I don't understand why it occurred in the first place."

James might laugh and say, "That's different. That should be different."

And so our conversations continued.

CHAPTER THIRTY-THREE

"You must find what's *true*, Dikkon. If one thing is true then the opposite can't be true. Two opposite things can't be true at the same time." This is one of Channa's most central tenets.

However, for me, the son of a poet, this tenet is a marriage-long conundrum.

"I love the strength of your logic," I offered.

"There's nothing about strength in this. It's just the way things are."

We were in the kitchen. Channa was wiping down the counters after dinner. I was trying to stay out of her way but be close. I had been away on a sales trip for three nights, and I especially liked to be close.

She said, "I've got a whole list of things to check off, to find out if they're true, and I'm checking them."

I laughed. "And once you get something checked, it stays checked."

"You're darned right."

"Not with me. Once I check something off, the next day I

go back and erase the check mark and need to start thinking it through all over again."

She smiled at me. "Waste of time."

"Come here," I said. I took her arm and pulled her close. "Yes, but it's why I can enjoy to keep doing the same thing over and over, every day—selling, selling, selling. And we benefit from that. So kiss me." She did, and that was fun. I murmured into her ear, "But I admire your tenacity for the truth."

"Do you?" she asked, vulnerably, pulling back a little and watching my eyes.

I paused. Then I said, "Yes, certainly." I smiled. "Not when it's directed at me, when you're mad. But yes. Yes, I do."

"I only get mad when I can't get a straight answer."

I nodded. "One thing this Christianity business is doing is it's helping with straight answers. Or straighter, at least."

"That's because it's true."

"It *shows* me what's true, anyway, and therefore gives an example of truth—in action, so to speak—and that teaches me how better to speak it."

Now Channa leaned her body more solidly on me, sighed. "Yes. I've noticed."

We kissed again.

When we broke apart, Channa went back to cleaning. I sat on one of the stools across the counter from her. "You know, I'm finding the Bible truer every day."

She nodded. "There's so much humanity in it. Those who just laugh at the Bible don't understand the value of so much humanity."

"Or they don't understand that we are all just needy humans after all; we can't help it. And that we need to be filled with

God, and that we can't fill ourselves by ourselves—even though we have tried so very hard and would really rather do it by ourselves, so we won't need to give up our stubborn desire to admire our own choice making . . . even when we so often get it wrong." My voice trailed off. "Complicated sentence," I said.

"Make it simpler, Dikkon."

"Simpler? Okay." I began ticking my fingers. "We need God. God is available to us, but only if we choose Him. To help us, He sent us His law. We grappled with His law as Jews for 1,200 years . . . and we got it almost right . . . almost. Turned out, though, we needed more help. We needed a demonstration that was above the law, even above the laws of nature. So what did He do? He sent us Himself—as one of us—which even we could see would be impossible to do unless He actually did it."

I paused, thought a bit, and then summed it up. "And when He came to us as one of us, He knew He would need to do the one single thing—the one absolutely impossible thing—that we can't do for ourselves."

"What's that?"

I looked at Channa. "There's only one absolutely impossible thing. Dad used to walk his way around it. He'd say that after fifty years of marriage, every question between him and Mom had been answered. But there was still one unanswered question: which of them would die first. Well, the one *impossible* thing that we humans *can't* do for ourselves is to live forever."

Channa turned from me, squeezed her sponge into the sink, and turned back. She was still, watching me. She could tell there was more, and so she waited.

"If I become a Christian—"

"You think you will?"

"I don't know." I walked around the counter and took her hands. "I'm beginning to see how it works, is all."

Still she was watching me. I said, "I'm finding the Bible truer all the time. And Pastor Dan's explanations about how it works. But all true? If it *is* all true, what choice do I have? But that's just such a big leap to make."

The kitchen was tidy. Channa and I walked to the living room and settled on the couch. We smiled at each other. Something big still hovered around us, but I had run out of words to say about the big thing, and Channa saw that, so after a bit she opened her book.

I shifted around so I lay on the couch with the top of my head pressed against the side of her thigh. Minutes passed. The big something stayed where it was, patiently, waiting for me to come back to it. Instead, I dozed; it had been a long and frustrating sales trip. Though mine was probably the best job in the world, there were times when, distinctly, it was no fun.

Later, Channa took a deep breath and let it out. She closed her book. "Dikkon," she said, "that's enough reading for tonight. I'm done."

"I might, you know."

"You might?"

"I don't know how to say this, but, yes, I might."

"The thing you and I are trying to find is the *true* answer. It must be a true answer—that is validated by faith, and by faith alone. And by fifty years of experience."

"Yes," I said, "maybe this is the true answer—but what about the children?"

"Dikkon, we're thinking about this. That's all."

"But . . ."

"We just do the best we can," Channa said. "And the rest is the business of God."

"Well, thank God for that."

PART FIVE

"Dikkon, do you believe that Jesus Christ is the Son of God?"

"Yes."

"Do you believe that He died for you to pay the penalty for your sin?"

"Yes."

"Do you believe that God will forgive you and accept Christ's death as payment for your sin?"

"Yes."

"Do you want to receive Jesus Christ as your Lord and Savior?"

"I do."

Oh, my God!

CHAPTER THIRTY-FOUR

Having been a teenage boy, I can attest that I know how to make a car skid. I learned how to make a car skid so that I would be able to make a car stop skidding, if ever I needed to. But, as I will now confess, it's much more fun to create a skid than it is to stop a skid.

Growing up in northern New Hampshire, we fellows made good use of iced-over ponds. For the sake of the spirit of my mother—who may indeed be reading over my shoulder—I can honestly say that I was one of the cautious ones who waited until the ice was eighteen inches thick before joining my pals as they edged someone's father's car out onto the pond's surface— and then gloriously made it skid.

That caution differed from my earlier insouciance when it came to ice travel. There is a story, famous in my family, of the time my mother drove past a local pond early in the winter and saw her ten-year-old son and his dog edging their way out onto the black surface of the new ice, on their bellies, inch by inch, with me holding the barrel of my cap pistol and cautiously tapping ahead of myself with its grip.

I remember my logic. Of course, I knew that it is possible to break through thin ice. Everyone said so. I understood that breaking through thin ice would be a bad idea. No good would come of it. For example, my mother would be mad at me, and, even worse, my father.

However, I had my dog, Rock, with me, who would go and bring help if needed, and I had my gun. Guns have two very good qualities. First of all, they're guns—enough said. Second of all, they make useful ice tappers.

Mom screeched to a stop, erupted from the car, and creased the very heavens with her fury. I was to come back on shore *this instant and not one instant later!*

With the illogic that I have since discovered is part of the makeup of mothers, Mom failed to accept my explanation. Not only did Mom fail to accept my explanation, she revealed her failure during her subsequent remarks. Her remarks were unnecessarily loud, and more to the point, they failed to display even a hint of thoughtful nuance.

In short, by banishing me from the ice that day, Mom ruined my science experiment.

Knowledge, as I had learned in school, and as I did my best to remind my mother at the time, is always a benefit. My experiment was designed to increase both my own knowledge and—as an added gift to the world—the knowledge of others as well. Just how far can a ten-year-old boy and a dog creep out onto a pond only partially covered with ice in early December in northern New England? Many people would like to know.

Now, thinking back on my experiment, I am not certain

that once I had discovered just how far I could go, I would, in fact, have published my new knowledge to the world at large. It's even possible that I might not have shared my finding with my parents. You can never quite tell with parents.

That same not-wanting-to-share is the way I felt one day in another December—many long years after my famous creep across the ice—in Pastor Dan's office. I had just answered yes to four questions he asked me and burst into tears.

He had burst into tears as well. We had jumped up and embraced each other and thumped each other on the back. Bawling, we had cried out a happy prayer.

What a sorry sight we were: a brave paratrooper and an ice creeper, sobbing!

I was shy, but I was glad. I was deeply, deeply glad. Suddenly, after months and years, *I got it!* I wanted to tell Channa, "*I get it!*"

But I wanted the fact otherwise to remain a secret.

You see, I'd just reached the very thinnest edge of the ice that I'd been creeping across for nine months, and I'd tapped one final time, and the ice had shattered, and I'd plunged.

*   *   *

Thirty-two and three-quarters years before that moment in Pastor Dan's office, Channa had asked me a question almost as ultimate as were the four questions of Pastor Dan. I was a coward back then. You know all about this. I had said to Channa, "What if I say I want to marry you?"

Her question, her earth-shaking question: "Do you?"

I was terrified to ask, "Will you?"

Suppose she said no. Suppose she said yes. I couldn't bear to have either answer out there, hanging on the wind.

My admiration of Channa was boundless. The strength of her character was profound. Her physical beauty was only part of her magnetism, as was her joy at life. With her help, I might have the strength to free myself of sinful passivity and fear, albeit masked, as I hoped it was, by charm.

When I left off being an academic and became a salesman, some friends and family were mystified. While there are many advantages in sales—freedom, being one—sales' biggest advantage for me was that every single day I was forced to stand up straight, to face the prospect squarely, to control my fear, and to ask for the order.

After Channa's question aboard our pretty ketch in Southwest Harbor, it took me three more months before I acquired the inner fortitude to bring out the contract, so to speak—to put the pen in Channa's hand, and to ask her to sign.

Thirty-two years passed. Then Pastor Dan asked me four qualifying questions. This time, I had no hesitation. With a flourish of my pen, eagerly, I said yes four times and signed over my soul to Jesus Christ.

But I didn't want to tell anyone. I wanted to keep this shining amulet in my pocket, like my very special chestnut, just for a while.

I was—saved.

I was—born again.

These words—which I had heard and read frequently during months of study and debate and trial—were . . .

Well, they were odd.

How does one say them in regard to oneself and not have them turn to sand in a dry throat?

I drifted out of Pastor Dan's office and gave his secretary,

Ruth, what must have been a crazy grin and floated through the outer doorway and into the parking area and into the car and down the road and turned at our drive and made my way between the snowdrifts to the door and into the house and wished Channa were there. She wasn't. She was in New York, at a conference center, keeping her credentials up to date by taking a series of professional appraiser education courses.

But I had a different credential to share.

The phone rang. "Hi, I'm on a break between seminars. How are you doing?"

"I did it."

"Did what?"

I just grinned that crazy grin as though she could see me.

"You did what?"

"I took Christ as my Savior."

"Dikkon! Dikkon, *really*?"

"It sounds so odd to say."

"Dikkon!" Her tone changed to frustration. "Oh—they're starting again in a few minutes. But I've *got* to talk about this."

I barked a short laugh. "Channa, I *get it.*"

"What happened? Just tell me quick."

"I was seeing Dan. We'd been talking for maybe two hours— you know us—and he said, 'Okay, are you ready for some questions?' and I said yes, and he asked the questions, and I said yes to each one, and—there I was."

"What were the questions?"

"I can hardly remember. That's odd, isn't it? It's all a buzz. Wait a minute, let me think. Do I believe that Jesus Christ is the Son of God? That was one, I think the first one. Do I believe He died to pay the penalty for my sins? Yes. And, let's see. Do

I believe that God will accept Jesus' death as payment for my sins? And there was another one. Oh! Of course. Do I want to take Jesus as my Savior?"

Channa was silent.

"Yes, that was it. Those were the questions. And there weren't any answers but yes. No equivocation. Just yes."

"Wow. How do you feel?"

"Stunned. It's the same as when I finish writing a book, and suddenly there's something there on the desk that was never there before, and I made it. It's the same as when the babies were born, and they were suddenly actually there, after all the waiting, and they were real. I feel ten feet tall and filled with air and not . . . Like I don't even have a body at this moment—I'm just air."

"I don't know what to say. Congratulations."

I laughed. "I don't know what to do. I want to keep it quiet for a little. It's so strange. Channa, I feel so free!"

"Oh, Dikkon, I'm so sorry. They're calling us back in. I'll call the minute this session's over. Dikkon, I love you!"

"You could come too."

"What?"

"You could come to Christ too."

"Oh, thank you. How nice of you. But I can't talk now. I really can't, but I love you."

"I love you, too."

"We'll talk about it soon. I mean it—real soon."

"I want us to be together."

"Me too."

"Good-bye, sweetheart."

We hung up.

I didn't know quite what to do. I stood in the kitchen with the phone in my hand. I wandered into the living room and sat down on the couch. I realized I still had the phone in my hand. Dimly, I thought I'd better call Pastor Dan and ask him to keep this strange event quiet for a bit.

"Oh, but I've already told a lot of people, Dikkon. If you thought before that we are a loving congregation, you just wait and see what happens to you on Sunday!"

And he was right.

EPILOGUE

If this were a Hollywood movie, it would end here.

But it did not end here.

Three months later, Pastor Dan asked Channa the same four questions. And like me, she said yes, yes, yes, and yes.

The three of us were in Pastor Dan's office. As Channa said her yeses, I was electric with joy. I was crying. Pastor Dan was crying. Channa, being Channa, was not. Instead she grinned at me and said, "Happy anniversary." And I remembered that it was, and it was.

Also it was Round Island—*times one million.*

In May, when our youngest child, Rosalind, was home from college, Channa and I were baptized together in the baptistery at Small Point. Many friends, among them some Jewish friends— which I took to be a particular beneficence—were there.

After our baptisms, Rosalind began frequent meetings with Pastor Dan. Rosalind is a woman of Mediterranean womanliness, and though she is the youngest of our children, she is not to be overlooked. She wears her heart on her sleeve. As she said to me, "I wanted to get to know this guy who took away my parents."

Later that summer, lying in bed one night, Rosalind, who at that point usually spent her wakeful hours struggling back and forth about Christianity—as a Jew, she encountered many of the same doubts and confusions as her mother and I had encountered—Rosalind suddenly found herself happy and calm. She found herself dreaming of the Christmases and Easters she, her children, and her husband would spend with Channa and me, at home, in Maine. *Oh*, she thought to herself with happy startlement, *I guess I must already be a Christian. How nice!*

(And she had an idea who that husband might turn out to be—a strong and thoughtful young Christian man from her college in Virginia—which idea has proven to be correct.)

Two days later, with her mother, in Pastor Dan's office, Rosalind answered four questions, and she was born again.

Shortly thereafter, when I was teaching the adult Bible class before services, Jenn, one of Pastor Dan's three daughters and Sam's Sunday school teacher, burst in. "Come quick!"

Not alarmed, because Jenn was grinning from ear to ear, but moving with urgency, I hurried to Sam's classroom. Channa had just arrived there from choir practice. Jenn prompted Sam, "Tell your father what you just told me."

"Jesus is my hero. I love him."

"You want to follow Jesus for your life?"

"Yes."

Complex theological statements are not among Sam's skills. He is a young man of utter honesty. He will not say he believes something until he does. He requires a long time to work complicated ideas into a concept that he is able to state simply. One of the gifts Sam has given his parents and his siblings is our experience of his plain, simple, and practical honesty.

"Yes," Sam said. "Yes, I do."

Lena and James, as Jews, explore the worlds—and the worldviews—to which they adhere. They continue to ask us questions.

There are precepts of evangelical Christianity that are off-putting to those who are not, at first, inclined to go this way. We know that.

One difficult precept is Bible-believing Christianity's certainty of its rightness. That certainty comes to the Christian only by the movement of the Holy Spirit within, and it comes only when the person has been called. Another difficult precept is doctrinal. How can there be predestination and free will at the same time? How does that *work*?

When Channa and I are asked, we do our best to explain.

*　　*　　*

My father and I—the two of us, we burned over the wrong things, and our flames drove us in different directions.

Dad took thirty years to recover from the death of his mother—he burned about it, and that burn, as he explained, kicked his verse into gear and drove him through a half century of literary prominence. As for me, for thirty-eight years, I burned at the guilt-stake of not warning others about an accident before it happened. In my imagination, I concocted fantastical conversations between the devil and me, elevating my youthful neglect of responsibility into a Job-like confrontation of biblical proportions that had cost me my soul.

Ah, poets.

And their sons.

Both Dad and I suffer from an innate tendency to elevate what are ordinary human occurrences into symbolic hyperbole. We do this, first, because we love the words that we can surround them with—how wonderful we find that creativity!—but, second, we do it because we are afraid that we might be just ordinary, flawed human beings after all.

I was sixty years old when I answered four questions from Pastor Dan and acknowledged that I am, in fact, just an ordinary, flawed human being after all. As an ordinary, flawed human being after all, I answered yes to Pastor Dan's four questions because I needed forgiveness and love of a greater nature—of a redemptive and a salvific nature—than what I received from my ordinary, flawed human-being father.

I needed forgiveness and love that comes only from our ultimate Father.

The difference between Dad and me is this. Dad delighted in Christian thought and in the poetic ecstasy that may arise from it and from the natural world that surrounds us. At the same time, he agonized about the power of death over our human desires. He asserted again and again that there is an equal struggle in the universe and in the human soul between the power of good and the power of evil. We are devil and angel, as he so often preached. We have the intelligence to yearn after redemption, but our intelligence sometimes blocks our success at finding it. Art—creating a beautifying answer while using our own creativity—art was the answer for Dad.

I, on the other hand—I knew myself to be eternally damned. It took me many years of increasingly strict Judaism before I was able to articulate this concept, even in my mind. It wasn't until Dad died and I was truly lost that I was compelled from outside of myself, one March morning in Maine, to cross the road and to learn I could be eternally saved. Then it took me nine months of intense study and testing to make my way to eternal salvation; yet then I was born anew.

Dad was a man who could hold two opposite truths in his mind at the same time; he was a poet. For him, that's how it worked. That's how he trained me. I was not at ease with that training, though I was habituated to it and though I loved my dad.

For me, at last, there is a single salvific statement, which now acts within my life.

God wins.

NOTES

1   *Premiere Generation Ink* 1, no. 1 (Winter 2000): 9–10.
2   Nigel Nicolson, *Portrait of a Marriage* (Chicago: University of Chicago Press, 1998), 202–03.
3   T. S. Eliot, *The Letters of T. S. Eliot, Volume 4: 1928–29* (New Haven, CT: Yale University Press, 2013), 39n3.